co-authored by

Norma Don   **Sharron Werlin Krull**

illustrated by

Amy Flynn

WHAT IS PLAY POWER?

PLAY POWER began with encouragement from parents and teachers who
desired quality enrichment experiences in movement for their children.
PLAY POWER continues as a class for young children and serves as a
resource for professionals in the Early Childhood Field.

Published by Play Power
Cover and interior illustrations by Amy Flynn
Typesetting & layout by Teresa Craft
Printing by Gall House Printing, Antioch, CA

Library of Congress Catalog Card Number: 94-92243
ISBN 1-885650-00-0 (pbk.): $14.95

Printed in the United States of America
First Printing 1986   Third Printing 1990
Second Printing 1988   Fourth Printing 1994

How to order:
Single copies may be ordered from Play Power,
1365 St. Catherine Court, Concord, CA 94521.
Quantity discounts are also available.

For information on keynotes, lectures, seminars, workshops and in-services with Sharron Werlin Krull, call (510) 680-4390.

 Dedicated to:
The spirit of Play Power in all
the young at heart

Grateful Acknowledgements:
Edward Don
Steven Krull
Corinne Nielson

Our students at:
Glorietta Elementary School, Orinda
Lafayette Community Center
The Orinda Pre-School
Orinda Community Center

And of course,
Andrea, Corrie, J.P., Juliet

TABLE OF CONTENTS

ABOUT THE AUTHORS

norma don

Multi-faceted and multi-talented best describe Norma and her wide range of personal interests. In the professional areas of Education, Parent Education, and Perceptual Motor Skills, Norma's special organizational flair has gained her a reputation for skill and innovation. She taught first grade for twelve years in the Fremont (California) Unified School District. As the motor skills instructor for Glorietta Elementary School in Orinda, California, she served on that district's Physical Education Curriculum Committee. Norma continues to teach PLAY POWER, the class she and Sharron first offered to children in 1980. They co-direct ORINDA KIDS' CAMP (since 1982). Norma teaches Kindergym at Lafayette. Sharron and Norma organized that successful facility and program and serve as Directors. Norma is a graduate of the University of California at Berkeley with a B.A. in Sociology and holds a California Life Teaching Credential for kindergarten through junior college. She and her husband Edward, daughters Juliet and Andrea, live in Orinda.

sharron werlin krull

Sharron has a charismatic enthusiasm that inspires and leads others in Early Childhood. She began with a B.S. degree in Elementary Education from Miami University of Ohio that took her to the public schools in Colorado before settling into a parent cooperative environment in a California preschool. Sharron has continued her education with graduate classes in Early Childhood as well as extensive training in Sensory and Perceptual Motor Development. Her inspirational high energy workshops and unique keynote addresses keep her in great demand throughout the nation. Sharron is the Director/Teacher at Creative Play Center and on staff as an Early Childhood instructor at a local community college. Sharron co-authored the favorite teacher resource, CIRCLE TIME ACTIVITIES FOR YOUNG CHILDREN and recently produced two videos, SHARIN' WITH SHARRON PRESENTS CIRCLE TIME and SHARIN' WITH SHARRON PRESENTS PLAY POWER. Sharron lives in Concord, CA with her husband, Steve. Together they have four children, J.P., Corrie, Christy and Marc.

ABOUT THE ILLUSTRATOR

amy flynn

Amy received her B.S. in illustration from San Jose State University in 1982, and promptly went to work for Hallmark cards. Two years with Hallmark was about all that she could stand, so she moved to England, where she completed the illustrations for PLAY POWER (her second book, after CIRCLE TIME). She's back now, and after spending six years as an artist for Current Inc. in Colorado Springs, she is now a freelance children's book and greeting card illustrator whose books include THE TEENY TINY FARM and NOAH'S ARK for Random House and TEDDY'S BUSY NIGHT, DOLL PARTY and THE BUNNIES' EASTER BONNET for Grosset & Dunlap. Amy was recently married, and has just moved, with her husband Phil, to an old house in Raleigh, North Carolina, which they are currently restoring.

INTRODUCTION

WHY IS THERE A NEED FOR THIS TYPE OF BOOK?

It is obvious that today's children benefit by exposure to a variety of learning situations. For *sensory* and *perceptual* input to be effective, children need stimulating and challenging experiences appropriate to their developmental level. *Perceptual* and *sensory motor* activities are basic to academic skills (reading, writing, spelling, mathematics).

It has been said,
"Thoughts which do not get into muscles,
never fully posses the mind."

Our goal is to return the focus to each child and his/her individual needs and abilities. We don't compare our differing abilities and past performances. We don't emphasize winning and losing. By eliminating stress associated with competitive sports, it is easy to foster an atmosphere of *cooperative play*. PLAY POWER is *cooperative play* consisting of games and activities that the children play together rather than against one another, just for the fun of it! Through this kind of play we learn teamwork, trust, and group unity. The emphasis is on total participation, spontaneity, sharing, the joy of play, acceptance of all players, playing our best, changing rules and boundaries to suit players, and recognizing that every player is important. Therefore, a major benefit of these success oriented activities is self-esteem!

HOW TO USE THIS BOOK?

Use this as a guide and modify it to your own needs and situation. Have enough confidence in your creativity to teach in a manner that is simple and comfortable for you. You will find that our WORDS THAT YOU NEED TO KNOW is a wonderful resource for carry through and expansion of all lessons. Be prepared to use it frequently.

WORDS THAT YOU NEED TO KNOW
(*italicized* throughout the book for easy reference)

Agility: quick, easy, lively movements.

Auditory discrimination: being able to hear and identify differences in sounds.

Auditory memory: recall and repetition of an auditory experience or activity.

Balance: being able to hold the position of the body through the interaction of muscles working together.
> *Dynamic balance*: when the body is moving
> *Static balance*: when the body is still

Bilateral: using both sides of the body at the same time in unison as in *jumping*.

Body image awareness: knowing and understanding the whole body and its parts and function; mental picture one has of ones own body that is the same as ones body concept.

Cooperative play: games and activities that the participants play together rather than against one another, just for the fun of it.

Coordination: parts of the body moving smoothly together.

Cross lateral: using different limbs on opposite sides of the body at the same time as in the ALLIGATOR CRAWL.

Dexterity: quickness, skill and ease in physical activity especially in using ones hands.

Directionality: the inner sense and knowledge of where things are in relation to the body (not the same as *laterality*).

Eye foot coordination: eyes and feet working together smoothly to meet a challenge.

Eye hand coordination: eyes and hands working together smoothly to meet a challenge.

Eye tracking: eyes being able to follow an object as the object moves in space.

Flexibility: ability to flex the body in various directions such as *turning* and *bending*.

Freeze: children cease all activity and direct attention to the *teacher*.

Imagery: formation of mental images by memory, imagination or fancy.

Kinesthetic awareness: inner messages from the muscles, tendons, and joints received by the body in order to move.

Large motor activity: (*Gross motor coordination*) involves use of the trunk and large muscles and limbs of the body.

Laterality: understanding of the differences between right and left and being able to control the two sides of the body independently and together. This is one of the earliest body awareness characteristics.

Leader: child designated by *teacher* to lead the activity.

Listening skills: ability to follow verbal directions.

Locomotor transport skills: body moves from one place to another by:
    walking: to move along on foot and advance by steps.
    marching: a precise type of walk, accompanied by lifted knees and swinging arms.
    leaping: an elongated step designed to cover distance or move over a low obstacle.
    running: moving rapidly so that for a brief moment both feet are off the groud.
    jogging: running at a slow pace.
    jumping: with both feet.
    hopping: on one foot.
    galloping: step-hop with one foot leading forward.
    skipping: series of step-hops done with alternate feet.
    tiptoes: balance on balls of feet and toes with heels raised.

Midline: center of the body vertically; dividing line between right and left sides of the body. The point at which the two sides of the body meet and are able to work at that point.

Non-locomotor skills: movement that does not involve transporting the body from one place to another, such as *bending, stretching, twisting, shaking*.

Perceptual motor: The ability to receive, interpret, and respond successfully to sensory information. Perception is the receiving or input system. Motor refers to the output or responsive movement.

Personal Space (*Individual space*): The amount of space needed for a person to make body movements without touching anything or anybody.

Ready position: children extend legs, cross at ankles and keeping bent knees in contact with the floor, bring legs into a true sitting position. This sitting position provides the greatest benefit to the child's development of good posture.

Sensory motor integration: messages from auditory, tactile, visual sources as well as the *kinesthetic* and *vestibular systems* resulting in appropriate physical activity.

Sit out: children not cooperating or participating in the activity are asked by the *teacher* to sit in a designated area of the space. Children resume activity when it is felt they can follow directions and cooperate with the rest of the group.

Small motor activity: (*Fine motor coordination*) use of the small muscles of the body (eyes, hands, fingers, toes) to perform specific small movements such as *rolling, throwing, catching.*

Spatial awareness: (*Spatial orientation*) coordinated movement in relationship to other objects in the environment.

Tactile stimulation: body learning from the sense of touch, skin contact and pressure.

Teacher: adult or person conducting the activities.

Unilateral: using one side of the body or one limb at a time.

Upper body strength: using arm and trunk strength to support the physical activity.

Vestibular stimulation (*Vestibular system*): stimulation within the inner ear resulting in equilibrium as with a sense of body position.

Visual discrimination: being able to see and identify differences.

Visual memory: recall and repetition of a visual experience or activity.

Visual motor planning: visual and motor responses working together in a smooth physical action.

4

TYPICAL LESSON OUTLINE

The *teacher* should show enthusiasm as the PLAY POWER lesson begins. <u>Shoes and socks are always removed</u>, except when the activity is out of doors. There are numerous safety reasons for barefeet in addition to the opportunity for *tactile stimulation*. Please note that the illustrations are fun and fanciful and do not reflect the authors' intentions (i.e., "children are barefoot" though accompanying illustration shows children in socks or shoes). Please plan your PLAY POWER lessons in accordance to the given environment.

Explain the day's main activity. The *teacher* should also discuss the equipment which will be used. At this time, it is appropriate to discuss past experiences with the same or similar equipment. We have found that a twenty minute period is most effective. This takes advantage of the attention span of young children.

Select a child to demonstrate the main challenge of the lesson. Proceed slowly to ensure that every child understands what will be involved with the PLAY POWER activity. Repeat the demonstration as many times as necessary. Children should be able to verbalize what their body will actually be doing.

The PLAY POWER lesson continues. Give all the children the chance to participate. But one should remember that children also are learning when they are watching. Encourage children to participate but do not force them to participate.

> Basic to having a good time with all PLAY POWER activities is for each member of the group:
> 1. to show consideration for others
> 2. to respect *personal space*
> 3. to take turns
> 4. to cease all activity upon hearing *freeze* from the *teacher*.

Children thrive with the familiar. Plan on repeating the activities and adding variation to them.

The goal of the closing is to have children focus and center on the day's accomplishments. This is a fine opportunity, also, for children to evaluate and to add their input to a PLAY POWER lesson.

HOW TO GET STARTED

This could also be called the <u>warm up</u> time. With young children any motor activity should begin with an opportunity to stretch and warm up muscles. Some winning warm up activities that we have used are the SUPER HEROES and GYMNASTIC JARGON.

SUPER HEROES (try to count to ten as you do each one)
1. SUPERMAN STRETCH: children attempt to keep their *balance* while up on *tiptoes* with arms stretched upward over their heads. The *teacher* could compare this to the Superman take off position for flying.
2. BATMAN BOUNCE: children find a spot (their "home") and *jump* (2 feet together). The *teacher* could indicate this is how Batman *jumps* into his Batmobile. Children are to stay in their own spot.
3. ROBIN RUN: again children find a spot. They will *run* in place. The *teacher* could compare this to Robin's *running* to catch up to Batman.
4. SPIDERMAN SWIVEL: children stand in a straddle (feet are shoulder width apart) firmly "planted in cement" (meaning feet do not move). Hands are placed on waist while children *twist* from side to side. This is like Spiderman moving on his web.
5. WONDERWOMAN WINDMILLS: This exercise should only be used with children age four and older. Children stand in a straddle with feet shoulder width apart, firmly "planted in cement" arms are stretched sideward. This activity will use the hand of one side of the body touching the foot of the opposite side. To accomplish this, the *teacher* must say, "*Turn*, touch toes, and up!" "Up!" means body is erect in a standing tall position. Repeat instruction.

GYMNASTIC JARGON: children like to use technically correct terms. These "warm ups" give the flavor of gymnastic-type activities. Note the similarity to the SUPER HERO exercises. We suggest each exercise to be repeated ten times.

1. STRETCH: children attempt to keep *balance* while on *tiptoes* with arms stretched upwards over their heads.
2. PIKE: with feet together, *bending* slightly at the knees (very important for back muscles), hands at waist, children *bend* at waist as their fingertips move from their waist downward to touch their toes.
3. SQUAT: children stand with feet at least a shoulder width apart, both hands on waist, upper torso erect and they *bend* their knees as the body is lowered while *balance* is maintained.
4. STRADDLE: children stand with feet at least a shoulder width apart. This seems very simple, but it is another type of *balance*. *Balance* is held until count of ten.
5. LUNGE: placing one foot in front of the other, toes are pointed straight ahead. As the back heel is on the ground, children *bend* front knee forward with both hands on it. This position should be held to a count of ten. Change feet and repeat.

CHAPTER ONE
LOW ORGANIZED GAMES

TITLES OF LOW ORGANIZED GAMES FOUND IN CHAPTER ONE

(Listed alphabetically with corresponding page number)

INTRODUCTION TO LOW ORGANIZED GAMES

BREAK THE ICE!... Get to know everyone in the group. With these games you can enhance feelings of enthusiasm as you create and sustain fun activities.

These games have been used with three year olds through ten year olds. They are enjoyable with younger children and have proven even more effective with older students. Between the two of us we work daily with preschoolers through third grade students.

Relays or team games often seem threatening to young children. Feelings of stress are inappropriate at this developmental level.

Low organized games can foster good feelings of self-esteem as children participate in a situation where success is a component of the activity. Everyone gets involved since every game in this chapter provides an opportunity for play without constraints of competition.

There will be requests to repeat these games. Because little or no equipment is needed, it is easy to be ready to play these low organized games often.

ALLIGATORS IN THE SWAMP

SET UP and MATERIALS:
1. Empty space (indoors or outdoors) with set boundaries.
2. Children need to know how to do ALLIGATOR CRAWL (p. 125).

PROCEDURE:
1. One child is in the middle of the empty space lying on stomach as the starter alligator.
2. Remaining children gather around this alligator and touch him shouting on command from the *teacher*, ALLIGATORS IN THE SWAMP.
3. Children then run within bounds of the alligator space while the alligator does the ALLIGATOR CRAWL trying to touch as many children as he can.
4. Children who are touched become alligators too.
5. Game continues until all children are touched. The last child touched becomes the new starter in the next game.

SPECIFIC GOAL:
1. *Cross laterality*
2. *Spatial awareness*
3. *Directionality*
4. *Vestibular stimulation*
5. *Cooperative play*
6. *Large motor activity*

SUGGESTIONS and VARIATIONS:
1. This game is effectively played in a space covered by mats as with two or three mats placed side by side making a very visible boundary. Children are not to stay on edge of mat for more than three seconds and must always try to run within the bounds of the alligator space.
2. ALLIGATORS IN THE SWAMP can be a nice follow-up to mat practice of the ALLIGATOR CRAWL (p. 125).

BARNYARD SALUTATION

NOTES

SET UP and MATERIALS:
1. Organize children sitting in *ready position* in a circle.
2. Discuss animals on the farm and each animal sound.

PROCEDURE:
1. Explain that a salutation is a greeting. In this game, as the animals meet, they will repeat their greeting three times.
2. Determine which animal you will be imitating for the entire game. Examples:
   a. Dog (p. 127): "Bow-wow, bow-wow, bow-wow"
   b. Frog (p. 131): "Ribet, ribet, ribet, ribet"
3. Choose two children who will then stand up from their spots, turn and face one another and assume the animal walk position needed. They will perform the selected animal walk moving toward one another. When they meet, they will give the salutation.
4. Then, they will stand up. They will fast *walk* (continuously moving forward around the circle) returning to their "original spot" or "home." They will enter the circle through their "home" going to the middle of the circle. The two participants will shake right hands, then, sit back down in their "original spot" or "home."

SPECIFIC GOAL:
1. *Locomotor transport skills*
2. *Laterality*
3. *Directionality*
4. *Spatial orientation*
5. *Cooperative play*

SUGGESTIONS and VARIATIONS:
1. This is an excellent game to give everyone a turn. A fast pace keeps and sustains the children's interest.
2. Other animal walk suggestions: RABBIT JUMP (p. 129), LAME DOG WALK (p. 128), etc...

11

SNICKERS AND HOOTS

SET UP and MATERIALS:
1. Empty indoor or outdoor space

PROCEDURE:
1. Children find a partner and partners stand back to back waiting to begin.
2. The *teacher* gives commands and partners react quickly while touching, for example:

   a. "Hand to hand"
   b. "Ear to ear"
   c. "Nose to nose"
   d. "Side to side"
   e. "Bottom to bottom"
   f. "Toes to toes"
   g. "Cheek to cheek"
   h. "Head to head"
   i. "Elbow to elbow"
   j. "Ankle to ankle"
   k. "Knee to knee"
   l. "Hip to hip"
   m. "Wrist to wrist"
   n. "Tummy to tummy"

3. The *teacher* gives commands in random order.
4. Whenever the *teacher* says, SNICKERS AND HOOTS, all the players must change partners. With the new partner, they stand "back to back" ready to listen. Play resumes.

SPECIFIC GOAL:
1. *Body image awareness*
2. *Listening skills*
3. *Tactile stimulation*
4. *Cooperative play*

SUGGESTIONS and VARIATIONS:
1. The *teacher* may give same command twice in a row to keep the players alert.

12

BIRTHDAY PARTY

NOTES

SET UP and MATERIALS:
1. One small object to represent a birthday candle.
2. Children standing in a line shoulder to shoulder with their hands behind their backs.

PROCEDURE:
1. *Teacher* explains that we all want to go to BIRTHDAY PARTY but we first must locate the "birthday person."
2. All children close their eyes while standing in the formation. *Teacher walks* behind each child touching their hands. This is a signal for the child to close his hands. Into the hand of one child goes the "birthday candle."
3. The "birthday person" is unbeknownst to the group. The *teacher* instructs the group of children to *walk* in the space (designated area for playing game) with their hands closed into fists. They must find the "birthday person" by going to each member of the group, one at a time, and asking this question: "Are you the birthday person?"
4. In reply to the question, hands are opened to show that they are empty or they contain "the candle." Upon viewing the candle, the questioner will *walk* to the area designated for "the party" and wait sitting in the *ready position.*
5. All children, including the child holding "the candle," ask "Are you the birthday person?" But only upon seeing the candle in the hand of the "birthday person" will a guest be able to go over to the "party area."
6. After everyone is at the "party," Happy Birthday To You will be sung.
7. Play continues with the "birthday person" selecting the next "birthday person" in the same way the *teacher* chose the first one.

SPECIFIC GOAL:
1. *Visual discrimination*
2. *Imagery*
3. *Cooperative play*

SUGGESTIONS and VARIATIONS:
1. After several plays, the teacher can call, *freeze* when there are about a dozen people at the party. Then, the "birthday person" is not revealed until the song is sung.

13

CONFUSION

SET UP and MATERIALS:
1. Empty space will depend on the size of the group.
2. *Teacher* gives signals with a triangle, or drum, or whistle.

PROCEDURE:
1. *Teacher* separates children into four equal groups standing shoulder to shoulder. Each group is a side of a square.
2. Groups facing each other are assigned the same signal (either one sound or two sounds of the triangle, drum or whistle).
3. Upon hearing their signal, the group will walk across to the opposite side of the square without body contact.
4. Children moving to the wrong signal or touching one another must *sit out* and miss one turn. They do this in the area that is identified for this purpose. After missing that one turn, they return to the players with whom they were standing.
5. After several practices to make sure each group moves only on their signal, introduce the signal three (making the signal three times). Since three is the sum of their signals (one + two), everyone moves to their opposite side thus creating true CONFUSION, as everyone moves.

SPECIFIC GOAL:
1. *Listening skills* combined with various *locomotor skills.*
2. *Spatial awareness*
3. *Cooperative play*

SUGGESTIONS and VARIATIONS:
1. Initially have children *walk*. But do try other challenges such as *jumping, hopping,* on *tiptoes,* etc...
2. Indicate that the signal four means nothing and that there should be no movement. You might try to "fool" them sometimes.
3. Add variety by trying "sideways," "backwards" and animal walks (pp. 125-134).
4. Take time to familiarize children with the other members of their group who share that side of the square with them.

14

BODY DRILL

SET UP and MATERIALS:
1. Tumbling mats placed on floor of room.
2. There should be enough mats so that each child has enough space without being crowded.

PROCEDURE:
1. *Teacher* gives commands and children quickly change body position on mats.
2. Here are some examples:
   a. "feet" (children stand upright)
   b. "seat" (everyone sits in *ready position*)
   c. "front" (laying on stomach with head at front edges of mat)
   d. "back" (laying on back with head at the back edge of the mat)
   e. "right side" (laying on the right side of the body and extending the right hand above the head)
   f. "left side" (laying on the left side of the body and extending the left hand above the head)
   g. "knees" (children on knees with the trunk of the body held upright)

SPECIFIC GOAL:
1. *Listening skills*
2. *Agility*
3. *Kinesthetic awareness*
4. *Body image awareness*

SUGGESTIONS and VARIATIONS:
1. Important: for safety avoid using command "knees" immediately following the command "feet."
2. Children should move quickly but they should never just "throw" themselves onto the mat.

15

NAME BALL GAME

NOTES

SET UP and MATERIALS:
1. Children sitting in a circle
2. One rubber utility ball

PROCEDURE:
1. Children say their name aloud just before *rolling* the ball to another person in the circle.
2. Encourage children to establish eye contact with one another so that they know when they will be receiving the ball.
3. This is a wonderful getting acquainted game.

SPECIFIC GOAL:
1. *Dexterity* is needed to *roll* the ball and to receive it.
2. *Eye hand coordination*
3. *Cooperative play*
4. *Small motor activity*

SUGGESTIONS and VARIATIONS:
1. With older children (five yrs. plus), stand up and bounce the ball from one person to another in the circle.
2. With older children (five yrs. plus), stand up and toss the ball under hand from one person to another in the circle.

ANIMAL PARADE

SET UP and MATERIALS:
1. Choose three sound makers (such as a tambourine, triangle, bell, whistle, etc...)
2. Recommend matted or carpeted area (at least a sixteen foot by eight foot area).
3. Position children along the long side of matted area, sitting down.

PROCEDURE:
1. Explain that each sound identifies a particular animal walk.
   For example: the bell represents the DOG WALK (p. 127)
                          the triangle represents the GORILLA WALK (p. 134)
                          the tambourine represents the ALLIGATOR CRAWL (p. 125)
2. *Teacher* should have a demonstration of each sound and the accompanying animal walk.
3. Upon hearing the sound, children will move to the opposite side of the matted area using the appropriate animal walk without body contact with one another.

SPECIFIC GOAL:
1. *Auditory discrimination*
2. *Directionality*
3. *Spatial orientation*

SUGGESTIONS and VARIATIONS:
1. Previous instruction with each animal walk should precede this game.
2. Use a signal that means nothing so when that signal is given, there should be no movement.

NO NAME BALL GAME

SET UP and MATERIALS:
1. Children stand in a circle equally spaced apart.
2. Seven inch or slightly larger utility ball
3. This game as described is best used with children of second grade age or older.

PROCEDURE:
1. *Teacher* begins play by bouncing the ball to any player.
2. This first player bounces it to a second player and the ball continues to be bounced to someone who has not had a turn.
3. The *teacher* calls out, NO NAME whenever it is to be returned to the *teacher*.
4. Then, the *teacher* must bounce it back to the original first player who must then continue the original sequence of players. The *teacher* can call out "NO NAME" and always expect the ball to be returned.
5. This game gets more difficult as more and more players get a turn. New players are added in sequence.
6. The last person to receive the ball must realize that he/she is the last person and call out "Stop!"

SPECIFIC GOAL:
1. *Visual memory*
2. *Small motor activity*
3. *Spatial awareness*
4. *Dexterity*
5. *Cooperative play*

SUGGESTIONS and VARIATIONS:
1. With younger children, the group could be sitting down so the ball could be *rolled*. This has been successful with first grade.
2. After direction #6 is reached, it is really fun to return the ball to the *teacher* and see if the entire sequence can be repeated without a break. In this event, the *teacher* never calls out NO NAME. You can see if everyone is alert and ready for the ball.

TOOTHPICKS

NOTES

SET UP and MATERIALS:
1. Children are standing in a straight line facing the *teacher*.

PROCEDURE:
1. The *teacher* gives commands to children. Examples:
    a. "stand on one foot"
    b. "hands in the air"
    c. "*jump* up and down"
    d. "put your finger on your nose"
    e. "*hop* on one foot"
    f. "touch your toes"
2. The children complete each direction and listen for the *teacher* to give the next command.
3. When the *teacher* gives command, TOOTHPICKS! all the children put feet together, arms at sides and stand as straight and tall as TOOTHPICKS.

SPECIFIC GOAL:
1. *Listening skills*
2. *Locomotor skills*
3. *Body image awareness*

SUGGESTIONS and VARIATIONS:

CROSSING THE SWAMP

SET UP and MATERIALS:
1. Indoor or outdoor space with start and finish boundaries.

PROCEDURE:
1. This is an activity involving imaginative play with physical movement. The *teacher* sets the scene by explaining that the children are at the start of the swamp. This special swamp is not always filled with water. Therefore, CROSSING THE SWAMP will change with each situation. Several children can cross at the same time if they respect one another's *personal space.*
2. The swamp can be filled with:
    a. eggs
    b. deep snow
    c. sticky tar or quick sand
    d. oil
    e. marbles
    f. glue
    g. worms
    h. crunchy leaves

SPECIFIC GOAL:
1. *Locomotor transport skills*
2. Creativity
3. *Imagery*

SUGGESTIONS and VARIATIONS:
1. Routine *locomotor skills* can also be used such as:
    a. *hopping*
    b. *jumping*
    c. *skipping*
    d. various animal walks (pp. 125-134)

JACK OR JILL RABBITS GO HOME

NOTES

SET UP and MATERIALS:
1. Empty indoor or outdoor space.
2. Children divided into groups of three scattered in the space.
3. One hoop for each group of three children.
4. Triangle or bell to be used for noisemaker.

PROCEDURE:
1. Two of the children in each group sit down in *ready position* facing one another on either side of hoop. The third child is the JACK RABBIT or the JILL RABBIT and is sitting in *ready position* safely inside of the hoop which is "home."
2. There should be extra "rabbits" and the *teacher* could break up a group of three so that entire group could be "rabbits."
3. The *teacher* explains that the RABBITS GO HOME by doing the RABBIT JUMP (p. 129). Several children should be asked to demonstrate.
4. When the *teacher* says, "Bang!" the "rabbits" do the RABBIT JUMP out of the hoop into another hoop. Whenever a JACK RABBIT or JILL RABBIT enters a home, the two children sitting around the hoop immediately stand up and join hands to provide a roof to protect their "rabbit."
5. At the sound of the noisemaker, everyone sits down. The game continues when the *teacher* says, "Bang!"

SPECIFIC GOAL:
1. *Spatial awareness*
2. *Directionality*
3. *Body awareness*
4. *Bilateral coordination*
5. *Dynamic balance*
6. *Cooperative play*

SUGGESTIONS and VARIATIONS:
1. This activity should be divided into approximately three equal time periods so that every child has at least one opportunity to be a JACK RABBIT or a JILL RABBIT.

GEIGER COUNTER

SET UP and MATERIALS:
1. Organize children sitting in a circle in *ready position*.
2. One bean bag

PROCEDURE:
1. Define a GEIGER COUNTER as a machine that locates precious metals.
2. A bean bag is identified as the precious metal, "gold."
3. A child is selected to be the first "prospector" seeking the gold.
4. The circle of children represents the GEIGER COUNTER and they will clap loud and fast as the "prospector" gets closer to the "gold." They will clap slowly and quietly when the "prospector" is far away from the "gold." Once the children understand this concept, then you can proceed.
5. The "prospector" is told to hide his/her eyes.
6. The *teacher* will place the "gold" (the bean bag) in the lap of a child.
7. The "prospector" will uncover his/her eyes and begin to circulate within the circle. Once the "prospector" starts *walking*, then the GEIGER COUNTER claps to help him/her find the "gold." The clapping gets loudest and fastest when the "prospector" stands directly in front of the person who is hiding the precious "gold."
8. When the "prospector" thinks he has found the "gold," he points to the child (who is thought to be hiding the bean bag) and shouts, "Eureka! I have found it!" If he has guessed incorrectly, he continues *walking* and *listening* until he is ready to make another guess.

SPECIFIC GOAL:
1. *Auditory discrimination*
2. *Cooperative play*

SUGGESTIONS and VARIATIONS:
1. The "prospector" is not to grab the "gold" out of anyone's lap.
2. The child who had the "gold" could be the "new prospector" while the "old prospector" could select the child who will hide the "gold."

FROGS AND FLIES

NOTES

SET UP and MATERIALS:
1. Empty indoor or outdoor space
2. Children are standing in a circle
3. Two balls of different color and/or size or one nerf (sponge ball) and one rubber utility ball.

PROCEDURE:
1. Identify one ball as the "fly." Discuss the way flies move and flit about. The other ball is identified as the "frog" and it must jump from spot to spot or from one person to the other in order around the circle.
2. Therefore, the ball that is the "frog" must move around the circle by being passed from person to person.
3. The ball that is the "fly" may be passed by tossing or bouncing in random order within the circle.
4. During an established time limit, see if the "frog" will catch the "fly" (by ending up next to it) or will the "fly" still be "flitting about." Even small children know that FROGS love to eat FLIES, so they take great pleasure in participating enthusiastically.

SPECIFIC GOAL:
1. *Eye hand coordination*
2. Maintaining attention
3. *Imagery*
4. *Cooperative play*
5. *Small motor activity*

SUGGESTION and VARIATIONS:
1. Depending on the size and the age of the group, set a reasonable three to five minute time limit per game.

23

FRIENDLY MUSICAL HOOPS

SET UP and MATERIALS:
1. Moderate amount of indoor or outdoor space.
2. Scattered in the space, one hoop per child.
3. Music: from records or tape recorders

PROCEDURE:
1. Each child sits in *ready position* inside a hoop.
2. *Teacher* starts music and child stands holding hoop at waist level *walking* around space.
3. When *teacher* stops music, child drops hoop to floor and immediately sits down in *ready position.*
4. Repeat this a few times before proceeding further.
5. Music starts and children stand up holding their own hoop at waist level and every one begins to walk around the space.
6. When the music stops, each child and another child close to him put their hoops together and the children are paired up so their hoops now make a stack of two on the floor.
7. When the music starts, both children hold stack of two hoops at waist level and *walk* around space.
8. The game continues now with the children working as partners dropping hoops when music stops and sitting down in *ready position.* Do this a few times before proceeding.
9. To change partners, repeat as from instruction #1 with one child in each hoop singly placed on the floor.

SPECIFIC GOAL:
1. *Spatial awareness*
2. *Listening skills* combined with various *locomotor skills*
3. *Directionality*
4. *Cooperative play*

SUGGESTIONS and VARIATIONS:
1. Use a variety of *locomotor* movements such as *skipping, jumping, tiptoes, galloping.*
2. FRIENDLY MUSICAL HOOPS is a good activity to use in conjunction with MERRY MUSICAL HOOPS (p.25).

MERRY MUSICAL HOOPS

SET UP and MATERIALS:
1. One hoop per child scattered in a moderate amount of space either indoors or outdoors.
2. Music: record or tape with appropriate machine.

PROCEDURE:
1. Each child stands beside a hoop.
2. The *teacher* starts the music and the children *walk* around the hoops making sure not to touch any of the hoops while the music is playing.
3. When the *teacher* stops the music, each child steps into the nearest hoop. More than one child in any one hoop is alright.
4. The *teacher* removes a hoop from the floor before resuming the music.
5. The game continues as before with the *teacher* stopping the music, the children stepping into the nearest hoop and the *teacher* removing yet another hoop.
6. MERRY MUSICAL HOOPS ends with one or two hoops on the floor. All of the children are working together ensuring that everyone finds a place inside a hoop. It is a bit crowded but a lot of fun.

SPECIFIC GOAL:
1. *Spatial awareness*
2. *Listening skills* combined with various *locomotor skills.*
3. *Cooperative play*

SUGGESTIONS and VARIATIONS:
1. Use a variety of *locomotor* movements such as *skipping, hopping, tiptoes, jumping, galloping.*
2. FRIENDLY MUSICAL HOOPS (p.24) can be a nice follow-up for MERRY MUSICAL HOOPS.

"NO THANK YOU!" BALL

SET UP and MATERIALS:
1. Children sitting in a circle
2. One rubber utility ball

PROCEDURE:
1. Children say their name aloud just before *rolling* the ball to another person in the circle.
2. Children try not to *roll* it to someone who has already had the ball.
3. If the ball is headed for someone who has already had the ball, then, that player says "NO THANK YOU!" An alert player near by who has not had the ball can then save the turn by stopping the ball.
4. The player who *rolls* the ball to someone who has already had the ball (without a save) is to *sit out.*
5. The *teacher* should stop the game when about two thirds to three fourths of the group has had a turn.

SPECIFIC GOAL:
1. *Visual memory*
2. *Auditory memory*
3. *Dexterity*
4. *Small motor activity*
5. *Cooperative play*
6. *Eye hand coordination*

SUGGESTIONS and VARIATIONS:
1. Standing up and bouncing the ball to each other.
2. For a young group of children refer to NAME BALL GAME (p. 16).
3. *Sit out* just means scooting a little back from the circle and the line of the ball.

OVER AND UNDER

NOTES

SET UP and MATERIALS:
1. Children divided into groups of equal number.
2. Seven inch rubber utility ball for each group.

PROCEDURE:
1. All children are sitting down in their squads.
2. The *teacher* demonstrates with one squad by having them form a straight line one person behind the other. The *leader* holds the ball.
3. The ball is then passed overhead from player to player. The last person receiving the ball quickly moves to the head of the line. This continues until the original *leader* once again stands at the start of the line.
4. The activity is repeated but this time, the ball is passed between the legs of the players.
5. The third time the activity is started, the ball goes overhead, then, the next person passes it between his legs to be passed overhead, thereby, OVER AND UNDER.

SPECIFIC GOAL:
1. *Small motor activity*
2. *Dexterity*
3. *Cooperative play*
4. *Eye hand coordination*

SUGGESTIONS and VARIATIONS:
1. Verbalize during the demonstration OVER AND UNDER.
2. The number of members in the squad should be appropriate to the age and ability of the children.
3. With younger children it is best just to play this game to direction #3.

27

"DOGGIE, DOGGIE DROP YOUR BONE"

SET UP and MATERIALS:
1. Organize children sitting in a circle.
2. Have a bean bag available.

PROCEDURE:
1. A player is chosen to be the "doggie" and stands up.
2. "Doggie" *walks* around the outside of the circle carrying the bean bag in his/her hand.
3. Before making a complete circuit, the "doggie" drops the bean bag in back of a seated player.
4. That player picks up the bean bag and attempts to reach the "doggie's" home (empty space around the circle where "doggie" was sitting) before "doggie" gets to that spot.
5. Player reaching "home" first continues game as "doggie."

SPECIFIC GOAL:
1. *Directionality*
2. *Locomotor transport skills*
3. *Agility*
4. *Cooperative play*

SUGGESTIONS and VARIATIONS:
1. Encourage each child playing to be given a turn.
2. Have children try moving around the circle using other *locomotor skills* such as:
   a. on *tiptoes*
   b. *galloping*
   c. *skipping*
   d. *jumping*
   e. *hopping*

PASS 'N COUNT

NOTES

SET UP and MATERIALS:
1. Divide children equally into at least two circles.
2. Six to eight players is an ideal size for each circle.
3. Seven inch diameter (or slightly larger) ball for each circle.
4. The *teacher* assigns the "magic number" and announces it.

PROCEDURE:
1. Designate a child to be the *leader* for each circle.
2. The *leader* of each circle holds the ball when the game starts.
3. On the signal "Go!" each circle will begin passing the ball from one player to another clockwise.
4. Each time the *leader* of the circle receives the ball, the *leader* will call out as the count is kept, "one around," "two around," etc... When a circle has reached the "magic number" that was designated by the *teacher*, the entire circle sits down.
5. Each circle tries to be the first to reach the "magic number" that the *teacher* designated. A good "magic number" is one that is close to the number of players in each circle.

SPECIFIC GOAL:
1. *Eye hand coordination*
2. *Dexterity* with a ball
3. *Small motor activity*
4. *Cooperative play*

SUGGESTIONS and VARIATIONS:
1. Have the children stand in a circle formation but facing sideways. Each player will look at the back of another player. They can pass the ball with these variations:
   a. overhead
   b. children *bend* over and ball is passed between knees
2. Standing in the circle formation the ball can be bounced from one player to the next if space permits.

GHOST GUARD

SET UP and MATERIALS:
1. One ball
2. One bowling pin ("the ghost")
3. Available indoor or outdoor space

PROCEDURE:
1. Children stand in a circle facing the center.
2. The *teacher* selects a child to be the GHOST GUARD who is to guard the "ghost" (the bowling pin) in the center of the circle.
3. Children in the circle attempt to knock down the "ghost" by *rolling* the ball at the bowling pin.
4. The player who successfully knocks down the pin becomes the new GHOST GUARD as play resumes.

SPECIFIC GOAL:
1. *Eye hand coordination*
2. *Dexterity*
3. *Small motor activity*
4. *Cooperative play*

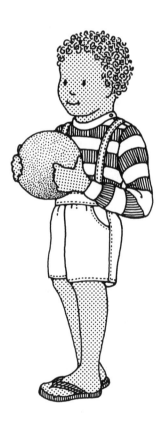

SUGGESTIONS and VARIATIONS:
1. For an older and larger group of children, divide them into squads. Assign each squad an opportunity to guard the pin for two minutes. Keep track of which squad guards the pin for the longest amount of time within the time limit.
2. You can use more than one ball.

PIRATES OF THE CARIBBEAN

SET UP and MATERIALS:
1. Available indoor or outdoor space
2. Four bean bags or nerf balls
3. If outdoors then set boundaries with ropes, cones or other markers into a large rectangular area

PROCEDURE:
1. Children position themselves in the space and wait for the signal to "start."
2. The *teacher* distributes bean bags or nerf balls (identified as the "pirates' poison") to four children (identified as the "pirates"). The "pirates" try to tag the remaining players on the shoulder as these players travel about the space. Each "pirate" tags only three players and to the third player gives up the "pirate's poison" (the bean bag or nerf ball). Thus, we have a new "pirate" and the old "pirate" is now travelling about the space (and subject to be tagged too).
3. The first two "travellers" tagged by a "pirate" are standing with feet frozen but arms doing a "swimming-like" motion. These players can be freed by any other "traveller" when the travelling player touches their shoe. They are, then, unfrozen and free to travel once again.

SPECIFIC GOAL:
1. *Spatial awareness*
2. *Visual motor planning*
3. *Agility*
4. *Imagery*
5. *Cooperative play*

SUGGESTIONS and VARIATIONS:
1. If space allows, players can *run*. But inside the confines of a room, this game should be a *walk* or fast *walk* activity.
2. Since the players are never depleted, everybody is always moving as they play the game...PIRATES OF THE CARIBBEAN can go on forever!

31

HOCUS POCUS

SET UP and MATERIALS:
1. Children stand in a circle facing the center but with their left hands extended into the center of the circle.

PROCEDURE:
1. *Teacher* selects a child as the *leader*.
2. The *leader* will count aloud, "one, two, three" as he *walks* around the inside of the circle. Then, with his own right hand, the *leader* will take the left hand of a player who is standing as part of the circle.
3. The *leader's* line grows as each new player takes the left hand of another player before the *leader* gets to "three."
4. Members of the circle stand and wait to have their hand taken.
5. When the *teacher* says, HOCUS POCUS! all hands are dropped and each player of the *leader's* line must return to his original spot on the circle before the *teacher* finishes counting, "one, two, three."

SPECIFIC GOAL:
1. *Spatial awareness*
2. *Directionality*
3. *Cooperative play*
4. *Listening skills*

SUGGESTIONS and VARIATIONS:
1. For a real challenge in *spatial orientation*, try to assemble in different formations and have the line move as a serpentine (as a snake would).
2. The larger the group, the more fun with the game HOCUS POCUS.
3. HOCUS POCUS! should be called when about three fourths of the circle has joined the *leader's* line.

MUSICAL BEAN BAGS

NOTES

SET UP and MATERIALS:
1. One bean bag per child
2. Moderate amount of indoor or outdoor space
3. Music: record or tape with appropriate machine

PROCEDURE:
1. Each child places a bean bag on his/her head.
2. The *teacher* starts the music and the children all *walk* around the space while *balancing* a bean bag.
3. If the bean bag falls off a child's head, he/she must *freeze.*
4. How a child "defrosts" and becomes free moving again:
   a. another player must come to help
   b. the helping player can hold onto his own bean bag (which is still on the top of his head)
   c. helping player picks up the fallen bean bag and hands it to the "frozen" player
   d. now, the child can position the bean bag securely on his head and proceed to move freely in the space.
5. Game ends when the music stops.

SPECIFIC GOAL:
1. *Visual motor planning*
2. *Spatial awareness*
3. *Dynamic balance*
4. *Cooperative play*

SUGGESTIONS and VARIATIONS:
1. If there are not enough bean bags for everyone, substitute bean bags with "paper wads" (crumpling a piece of paper into a ball).

33

STOP THE MUSIC

SET UP and MATERIALS:
1. Available indoor or outdoor space.
2. Source of music such as tape recorder or record player

PROCEDURE:
1. The *teacher* explains that this is a *listening* game. During the playing of the music, children are to move around the space without touching each other showing that they respect *personal space.*
2. When the music stops, the children are to *freeze* in their spots.
3. They resume moving when the music starts again.
4. Use alot of positive reinforcement when someone follows the directions well. This will probably eliminate the need to have children *sit out* because they did not *freeze* when they were supposed to *freeze.*

SPECIFIC GOAL:
1. *Listening skills*
2. Various *locomotor transport skills*

SUGGESTIONS and VARIATIONS:
1. Typical movement challenges might be:
   a. *skip* in the space
   b. *tiptoe* around
   c. *hop*
   d. *jump*
   e. various animal walks (pp. 125-134)

RODEO ROUND UP

NOTES

SET UP and MATERIALS:
1. Empty space (indoors or outdoors) with set boundaries.

PROCEDURE:
1. One child who is designated as the "cowboy" or "cowgirl" stands in the middle of the empty space.
2. The other children are the "horses" and stand at/or behind one of the boundaries which were identified.
3. The "cowboy" or "cowgirl" says, "All Horses *Run!*" and children who are the "horses" *run* toward the other set boundary and the "cowboy" tries to touch as many of the "horses" as possible.
4. If the "cowboy" or "cowgirl" touches a "horse" that child, then, also becomes a "cowboy" or "cowgirl", and tries to touch the "horses" as they go from boundary to boundary. Each time the "cowboys" say, "All Horses *Run!*" so the "horses" know to start *running* toward the set boundary.
5. RODEO ROUND UP continues until all the children are touched. The last child touched becomes the new "cowboy" or "cowgirl" and starts the new game.

SPECIFIC GOAL:
1. *Spatial awareness*
2. *Directionality*
3. *Cooperative play*

SUGGESTIONS and VARIATIONS:
1. The "touch" should not be heavy handed.
2. The "cowboy(s)" or "cowgirl(s)" should give the command, "All Horses *Run!*"

35

SARDINES

SET UP and MATERIALS:
1. One bean bag
2. Children standing in a line shoulder to shoulder with their hands in back of them. They are the line of SARDINES.
3. Identify the child who will be the "fisherman."

PROCEDURE:
1. Explain that the "fisherman" is looking for the "treasure" (the bean bag). But the SARDINES are hiding the "treasure."
2. The "fisherman" stands in front of and facing the line. The *teacher* stands in back of the line.
3. Play begins with the "fisherman" covering his eyes as the *teacher* places the "treasure" (the bean bag) in the hands of a SARDINE.
4. The "fisherman" uncovers his eyes when the *teacher* says, "Pass!" the "treasure" is passed from one SARDINE to another in any direction the players choose.
5. The *teacher* says, "Stop!" The passing of the "treasure" stops. Then, the "fisherman" tries to name the player who has the bean bag.

SPECIFIC GOAL:
1. *Visual discrimination*
2. *Eye tracking*
3. *Dexterity*
4. *Small motor activity*
5. *Cooperative play*

SUGGESTIONS and VARIATIONS:
1. Try this game with the children sitting down in the line; the "fisherman" must also sit down too.
2. Have two bean bags (of different colors). Assign a "fisherman" for each color.

LOST SPACESHIP

NOTES

SET UP and MATERIALS:
1. Available indoor or outdoor space large enough to accommodate the entire group as they move.
2. Organize children to stand in a circle holding hands.

PROCEDURE:
1. The *teacher* selects two children. The two children hold hands and are now identified as the LOST SPACESHIP.
2. The LOST SPACESHIP must *walk* around the circle of children who are now known as the "mother ship."
3. The LOST SPACESHIP wants to come home and touches the clasped hands of two players.
4. The LOST SPACESHIP continues holding hands *walking* quickly around the circle ("mother ship") again. The two players whose hands were touched also continue holding hands and *walk* in the direction opposite to that of the LOST SPACESHIP.
5. The first pair to return and close the circle of the "mother ship" remain with the "mother ship" and the other two children resume play as the LOST SPACESHIP.

SPECIFIC GOAL:
1. *Directionality*
2. *Locomotor transport skills*
3. *Cooperative play*

SUGGESTIONS and VARIATIONS:
1. Children naturally tend to want to close the circle once it has been broken. Caution them that the circle can only be closed by the first pair of players (the LOST SPACESHIP) going completely around the "mother ship" (the circle).
2. Once children are familiar with the routine, introduce other *locomotor skills* such as *skipping, jogging, galloping. Running* is not suggested.

HIT THE DECK

SET UP and MATERIALS:
1. Tumbling mat placed in center of room
2. Children scattered around the room

PROCEDURE:
1. *Teacher* gives commands to children and they react quickly as members of the "Ship's Crew."
   a. HIT THE DECK! (children sit in *ready position* on the mat)
   b. "Galley!" (children form a straight line standing up with toes touching the front edge of the mat).
   c. "People Overboard!" (children assume the CRAB WALK position (p. 132) with weight on hands and feet, stomach facing up, anywhere on the floor except on the mat).
   d. "Lifeboats!" (children go sit against the wall on the left side of the room).

SPECIFIC GOAL:
1. *Listening skills*
2. *Spatial awareness*
3. *Agility*
4. *Cooperative play*

SUGGESTIONS and VARIATIONS:
1. *Teacher* may give same command twice in succession to keep players alert.
2. Establish a *sit out* area for children who do touch each other. Children who do touch each other may return after missing one turn or whatever the *teacher* explains at the beginning of HIT THE DECK.

SQUIRRELS IN THE TREES

NOTES

SET UP and MATERIALS:
1. Empty indoor or outdoor space.
2. Children divided into groups of three.

PROCEDURE:
1. Two children join hands and form a tree. The third child is the SQUIRREL IN THE TREE. Extra "squirrels" are located within the space though not in any "trees."
2. The *teacher* calls out, "*Run* squirrels!" All "trees" raise their arms while all "squirrels" attempt to relocate in a tree.
3. After several turns, rotate children so every child has a chance to be a SQUIRREL IN THE TREE.

SPECIFIC GOAL:
1. *Spatial awareness*
2. *Directionality*
3. *Body awareness*
4. *Agility*
5. *Cooperative play*

SUGGESTIONS and VARIATIONS:
1. Use other *locomotor skills* to get from one "tree" to another such as: *skipping, tiptoes, jumping*, various animal walks (pp. 125-134).

WHISTLE STOP

SET UP and MATERIALS:
1. Whistle
2. Large amount of indoor or outdoor space
3. Markers to set boundaries

PROCEDURE:
1. Scatter the children around the space.
2. On signal, "*Run!*" from the *teacher*, the children *run* in any direction until the whistle blows and then they must stop immediately.
3. They start again on signal, "*Run!*"
4. Encourage the children to *run* and stop on appropriate signals.
5. Children should stay within boundaries and avoid other players.
6. Establish a *sit out* area for players who do touch. They should lose just one turn before rejoining the group play.

SPECIFIC GOAL:
1. *Listening* and *locomotor transport skills*
2. *Spatial awareness*

SUGGESTIONS and VARIATIONS:
1. The children could add more movements upon hearing the whistle blow. For example: they could stop and clap their hands.
2. Instead of *running*, here are other possibilities:
    a. *walk* like an elephant
    b. *skip*
    c. *run* sideways
    d. *run* in a circle
    e. *hop* or *jump* to the right or to the left

EXERCISE FAMILY

NOTES

SET UP and MATERIALS:
1. Available indoor space
2. Record and record player or tape and tape recorder with two minute (maximum amount of time) selection.

PROCEDURE:
1. Gather children in sitting circle. Have children count off as "oranges," "apples" and "bananas."
2. "Oranges" are to stand up, leave the circle and scatter in the available space.
3. "Apples" go and stand toe to toe with an "orange."
4. "Bananas" go join the "orange/apple" couples to create an EXERCISE FAMILY: "orange, apple, banana."
5. Indicate that the "oranges" will exercise first (such as doing jumping jacks). The "apples" will keep count of the number of completed jumping jacks. The "bananas" will be the "cheerleaders" and cheer encouragement as the "orange" is exercising.
6. "Oranges" will exercise for the length of the song. Then, the song will be repeated twice more so that each person in the "family" will have a chance to exercise, to keep count, and to be the "cheerleader."

SPECIFIC GOAL:
1. *Cooperative play*
2. *Large motor activity*

SUGGESTIONS and VARIATIONS:

41

FIND THE BELL

SET UP and MATERIALS:
1. Children sitting in a circle
2. Small bell

PROCEDURE:
1. Players with hands behind their backs sit in *ready position.*
2. A child is selected to be the "detective" and sits in the middle of the circle covering his or her eyes.
3. Another child *walks* around the circle and places the bell in the player's hand.
4. *Teacher* announces, "Start!" The "detective" uncovers his or her eyes and everyone in the circle moves their arms up and down behind their backs (pretending to have the bell).
5. The "detective" listens for the sound of the bell so he/she can identify who is actually holding the bell. Modify the number of guesses appropriate to the age group.
6. The "detective" chooses the next "detective" (who assumes the *ready position* in the middle of the circle with eyes covered).
7. The person who held the bell now passes it to another player as in instruction #3 and the play resumes.

SPECIFIC GOAL:
1. *Auditory discrimination*
2. *Cooperative play*

SUGGESTIONS and VARIATIONS:

42

CATERPILLARS AND COCOONS

SET UP and MATERIALS:
1. Available indoor or outdoor space
2. Children divided into groups of three scattered in the space

PROCEDURE:
1. The *teacher* explains to the children that the "caterpillars" need to find the safety of their "cocoons." "Caterpillars" will move to the "cocoons" by using the CREEPING movement (p. 126). The *teacher* should have several children demonstrate CREEPING.
2. Two of the children in each group sit down in *ready position* and join hands. The third child is outside in the space. There should be extra "caterpillars" or the *teacher* could break up a group of three and that entire group could be called "caterpillars."
3. When the *teacher* calls, "creepy caterpillars," the two children forming any "cocoon," should raise their hands and lower them when a "caterpillar" has entered their "cocoon."
4. "Caterpillars" move from "cocoon" to "cocoon" using the CREEPING movement.

SPECIFIC GOAL:
1. *Agility*
2. *Spatial orientation*
3. *Directionality*
4. *Body awareness*

SUGGESTIONS and VARIATIONS:
1. This activity should be divided into approximately three equal time periods so that every child has at least one opportunity to be a "caterpillar."

CHAPTER TWO
PARACHUTE ACTIVITIES

45

TITLES OF PARACHUTE ACTIVITIES FOUND IN CHAPTER TWO

(Listed alphabetically with corresponding page number)

INTRODUCTORY LESSON

SET UP and MATERIALS:
1. Parachute in available indoor or outdoor space.

PROCEDURE:
1. Position children at the seams of the parachute sitting at *ready position.*
2. Discussion:
   a. What is a parachute?
   b. Where is a parachute usually used?
   c. How does the fabric feel?
   d. Identify the seams or ribs of the parachute.
   e. Identify the aperture or center hole of the parachute.
3. Show the children how to hold the parachute: GRIP
   a. From the edge, roll the parachute three times
   b. Claw Hold: This grip has the fingers down on either side of the seam with thumbs under the parachute, knuckles showing above the parachute. This is the most frequent grip and is known as the claw hold grip in our parachute lessons.
4. Safety reminders:
   a. Institute the *freeze* rule which means that at the *teacher's* direction, *Freeze!* the children cease all activity to listen to directions.
   b. Children stay away from the center hole or aperture of the parachute. This rule is very important as body parts should never get entangled in the aperture or center hole of the parachute.
   c. Stress working together in a cooperative spirit.
   d. Stress good listening.

SPECIFIC GOAL:
1. To inform children of the safe use of this piece of equipment so that the fun of these lessons can be enhanced.

SUGGESTIONS and VARIATIONS:
1. These activities are a good beginning for each parachute lesson. They serve to review and to remind.

SHAKING THE PARACHUTE

SET UP and MATERIALS:
1. Parachute in available indoor or outdoor space.

PROCEDURE:
1. Position the children at the seams of the parachute sitting at *ready position.*
2. The children assume the claw hold grip.
3. The *teacher* says, "Shake!" and the children SHAKE THE PARACHUTE up and down using elbow and arm extensions.
4. On command, *Freeze!* the children stop.
5. Ask the children to stand up. When they are standing, the *teacher* directs them to try not to move their feet. "Keep your body still and let your arms move up and down," is a good reminder.
6. Either standing or sitting, the children can try to SHAKE THE PARACHUTE with a side to side motion as a variation.
7. The *teacher* should instruct the children to vary this speed of the shaking and make allusions to moving like the "wind" or the "ocean waves."

SPECIFIC GOAL:
1. To provide specific practice in SHAKING THE PARACHUTE.
2. *Cooperative play*
3. *Large motor activity*

SUGGESTIONS and VARIATIONS:
1. It is always a good idea to review this activity before beginning any parachute lesson.

POP THE BUBBLY

SET UP and MATERIALS:
1. Parachute in available indoor or outdoor space.
2. Children are barefoot (if indoors).

PROCEDURE:
1. Position the children at the seams of the parachute sitting in *ready position.* The children grasp the parachute with the claw hold grip.
2. Select one child to demonstrate CREEPing on his seam. The *teacher* explains that by CREEPing around and about on the parachute we will be able to POP THE BUBBLY! However, the entire group must know how to do the CREEP (p. 126).
3. Several children are given the opportunity to CREEP around and about on the parachute. The children sitting down will need to SHAKE THE PARACHUTE up and down when the *teacher* says, "Shake!" After two minutes, the *teacher* calls out *Freeze!* so that each child on the parachute can return to their spot, sitting in *ready position* and new children can be selected to CREEP on top of the parachute to POP THE BUBBLY.

SPECIFIC GOAL:
1. *Balance*
2. *Directionality*
3. *Tactile stimulation*
4. *Cooperative play*
5. *Large motor activity*

SUGGESTIONS and VARIATIONS:

PARACHUTE

LOG ROLLING

SET UP and MATERIALS:
1.   Parachute in available indoor or outdoor space.

PROCEDURE:
1.   Position children at the seams of the parachute sitting in *ready position* with their shoes off.
2.   Demonstrate with one child the LOG ROLL (P.124) with his or her body lying across a seam of the parachute.
3.   The "logs" (the children) roll toward the center and at a signal from the *teacher*, return by LOG ROLLING to the starting spot.
4.   The children who are not "logs" SHAKE THE PARACHUTE up and down using the claw hold grip.
5.   Suggest that while the children are LOG ROLLING, they should try to get out the "wrinkles" on the parachute. This means they could be "ironing out" the parachute as they do the LOG ROLL.

SPECIFIC GOAL:
1.   *Tactile stimulation*
2.   *Body image awareness*
3.   *Agility*
4.   *Vestibular stimulation*
5.   *Cooperative play*
6.   *Large motor activity*

SUGGESTIONS and VARIATIONS:
1.   Begin with one or two children LOG ROLLING on the parachute. Repeat adding a few more children each time until there's a maximum of six to eight at a time on the parachute.
2.   Crooked LOG ROLLING should be corrected. Straight arms and straight legs keep the "log" rolling straight.

ALLIGATOR SNACK TIME

SET UP and MATERIALS:
1. Parachute in available indoor or outdoor space.

PROCEDURE:
1. Children are positioned at the seams of the parachute sitting in *ready position* with their shoes off.
2. Ask one child to demonstrate the ALLIGATOR CRAWL (p. 125) on the seam in front of him. He should do the ALLIGATOR CRAWL all the way on his seam to the center of the parachute. The center spot can be called the "snack bar." The "alligator" enjoys a "snack" (i.e. fishes, eels, etc...) and returns to his starting position still using the ALLIGATOR CRAWL.
3. After this demonstration (depending on the size of the parachute), assign several alligators at once. Provide each child with a turn.
4. Children who are not "alligators" SHAKE THE PARACHUTE up and down, holding with the claw hold grip while sitting down. Remind the children to sit in *ready position.*

SPECIFIC GOAL:
1. *Cross laterality*
2. *Tactile stimulation*
3. *Cooperative play*
4. *Large motor activity*

SUGGESTIONS and VARIATIONS:
1. "Alligators" can CRAWL under the parachute instead of on the parachute seam.
2. Or, participants all stand, inflate the parachute while the "alligators" CRAWL underneath the parachute.

51

WALK THE LINE

SET UP and MATERIALS:
1. Parachute in available indoor or outdoor space.

PROCEDURE:
1. Position the children at the seams of the parachute sitting in *ready position*. The children grasp the parachute with the claw hold grip.
2. Select one child to demonstrate *walking* on his seam. This is WALK THE LINE. The child should *walk* on the seam to the aperture (center spot), turn around and return.
3. After WALKING THE LINE, encourage the children to try to *walk* heel-toe. After this demonstration (depending on the size of the parachute), assign several children to WALK THE LINE at the same time. Try to provide a turn for each child.
4. The children who are sitting down will need to SHAKE THE PARACHUTE up and down upon hearing the *teacher* say, "Shake!"

SPECIFIC GOAL:
1. *Dynamic balance*
2. *Directionality*
3. *Eye foot coordination*
4. *Tactile stimulation*
5. *Cooperative play*

SUGGESTIONS and VARIATIONS:
1. "Brave the Waves": with this variation, the children *walk* around randomly on the parachute while others SHAKE THE PARACHUTE.

CRAB WALK, CAKE WALK

SET UP and MATERIALS:
1. Parachute in available indoor or outdoor space

PROCEDURE:
1. Position children sitting at the seams of the parachute in *ready position* holding the parachute with the claw hold grip.
2. Ask two children across from each other to let go of the parachute. These two children will CRAB WALK (p.132) on the parachute and exchange places. To encourage them to do a good CRAB WALK explain that they are delivering "cakes" on their flat stomachs to the new location. They will begin at the *teacher's* direction, CRAB WALK, CAKE WALK.
3. Other children will follow the *teacher's* instruction to SHAKE THE PARACHUTE until the "crabs" reach their new destinations.
4. Children can continue the game by having the "old crabs" select the "new crabs." Encourage them to choose people who have not already had a turn.

SPECIFIC GOAL:
1. *Directionality*
2. *Spatial awareness*
3. *Cooperative play*
4. *Large motor activity*
5. *Imagery*

SUGGESTIONS and VARIATIONS:
1. Have four people exchange places and the fun is even greater.
2. Children love to hear challenges like "Crabs delivering cakes." The imagery and language experiences can be very delightful.

53

STARFISH

SET UP and MATERIALS:
1. Parachute in available indoor or outdoor space.

PROCEDURE:
1. Position children at the seams of the parachute standing up and holding the parachute with the claw hold grip at waist level.
2. Ask five children to let go of the parachute. These five children are to lie on their backs with their heels under the aperture of the parachute. These children will resemble the "arms" of a STARFISH.
3. On the *teacher's* command, "Shake!" the other children SHAKE THE PARACHUTE up and down on the STARFISH for a minute or so. This gives the sensation of an ocean current or wave.
4. Repeat this activity to allow each child in the group a chance to experience the sensation of being part of a STARFISH.

SPECIFIC GOAL:
1. *Tactile stimulation*
2. *Cooperative play*
3. *Imagery*

SUGGESTIONS and VARIATIONS:
1. This activity is especially effective when accompanied by appropriate music or "ocean" sound effects.

TRAVEL

SET UP and MATERIALS:
1. Parachute in available indoor or outdoor space.

PROCEDURE:
1. Position children sitting in *ready position* at the seams of the parachute holding the parachute with the claw hold grip.
2. Ask two children across from each other to let go of the parachute. These two children will exchange places, *walking* on their seams of the parachute, crossing the aperture, and continuing their travel on the seam to their new location. The command TRAVEL! from the *teacher* will be the signal for both children to begin their *walks*.
3. The other children will follow the *teacher's* instruction to vigorously SHAKE THE PARACHUTE.
4. The *teacher* will select two new people and attempt to provide opportunities for everyone to TRAVEL who want to TRAVEL.

SPECIFIC GOAL:
1. *Directionality*
2. *Spatial awareness*
3. *Cooperative play*

SUGGESTIONS and VARIATIONS:
1. This is a wonderful activity for every participant who so desires to have a chance to TRAVEL to a new location.
2. Have two to four children participate at a time.
3. Other possible modes of TRAVEL:
   a. *Tiptoe*
   b. *Jump*
   c. Animal walks (pp. 125-134)

55

FIND YOUR HOME

SET UP and MATERIALS:
1. Parachute in available indoor or outdoor space

PROCEDURE:
1. Position children at the seams of the parachute sitting in *ready position* with their shoes off.
2. Children need to look on either side of them to establish who their neighbors are.
3. Demonstrate with one child the path he will take around the outside of the parachute (behind the backs of the sitting players) to get back to his "home."
4. On the *teacher's* direction, "*Walk!*" The child will *walk* around the outside of the parachute to return safely to his "home." Meanwhile, the other participants are sitting down around the parachute, using the claw hold to SHAKE THE PARACHUTE up and down.
5. Upon returning "home," the child sits in *ready position.*
6. It is especially enjoyable when several children at the same time are travelling to find their "homes." Be sure to specify that everyone travels in the same direction using the same locomotor skill.

SPECIFIC GOAL:
1. *Spatial awareness*
2. *Directionality*
3. *Cooperative play*

SUGGESTIONS and VARIATIONS:
1. Move around the parachute using other locomotor movements:
   a. *Gallop*
   b. *Jump*
   c. *Skip*
   d. *March*
   e. On *tiptoes*
   f. Animal walks (pp.125-134)

LIFT: "HI AND HELLO"

SET UP and MATERIALS:
1. Parachute in available indoor or outdoor space

PROCEDURE:
1. Position children at the seams of the parachute standing up and holding the parachute with the claw hold grip.
2. The *teacher* directs the children to touch the parachute to their toes.
3. The *teacher* says, "Lift!" and the children lift the parachute (using straight arms) up and over their heads (holding on at all times to the parachute).
4. As the parachute deflates, the children position the parachute at their "tummy button" (waist level). The *teacher* also says, "Down to your waist."
5. Several repetitions of this activity are effective for the children can greet one another as they see one another when the parachute is lifted.

SPECIFIC GOAL:
1. *Flexibility*
2. *Cooperative play*
3. *Large motor activity*

SUGGESTIONS and VARIATIONS:
1. Encourage children to greet one another verbally with a "HI AND HELLO." On repetition of this activity, direct the group to greet friends that they have not acknowledged before.
2. With older children, suggest they wave with their right hand or left hand.

PARACHUTE

57

UMBRELLA

SET UP and MATERIALS:
1. Parachute in available indoor or outdoor space.

PROCEDURE:
1. Position the children standing at the seams of the parachute holding it with the claw hold grip.
2. The *teacher* gives directions to the children.
   Here are some suggestions:
   a. "Stand on one foot."
   b. "Hands on your tummy."
   c. "*Jump* up and down."
   d. "*Hop* in place."
   e. "*Run* in place."
   f. "Touch your toes."
   g. "Touch your knees."
3. The children complete each direction always holding onto the parachute with the claw hold grip and listening for the *teacher* to give her next command.
4. When the *teacher* says, UMBRELLA! all the children put both hands and arms straight up in the air and they stand with their feet together as tall as possible.

SPECIFIC GOAL:
1. *Listening skills*
2. *Locomotor skills*
3. *Cooperative play*
4. *Large motor activity*

SUGGESTIONS and VARIATIONS:
1. The *teacher* needs to plan her commands to make sure that the children can do them while holding onto the parachute.
2. UMBRELLA command should be issued every third or fourth time to keep the children alert.

MUSHROOM

SET UP and MATERIALS:
1. Parachute in available indoor or outdoor space.

PROCEDURE:
1. Position the children at seams of parachute standing up and holding the parachute with the claw hold grip.
2. At the *teacher's* direction, "Lift!" the children lift the parachute and quickly *walk* forward toward the center of the inflated chute, looking up at the MUSHROOM cap above them.
3. As the parachute deflates, children quickly *walk* back to their original positions still holding onto the parachute.

SPECIFIC GOAL:
1. *Cooperative play*
2. *Imagery*
3. *Large motor activity*

SUGGESTIONS and VARIATIONS:
1. FROZEN MUSHROOM (p. 60) is a good follow up activity.

FROZEN MUSHROOM

SET UP and MATERIALS:
1. Parachute in available indoor or outdoor space

PROCEDURE:
1. Position children at seams of parachute standing up holding the parachute with the claw hold grip.
2. At the *teacher's* direction, "Lift!" the children lift the parachute and quickly *walk* forward toward the center of the inflated parachute looking up at the "mushroom cap" above them.
3. At the *teacher's* commands, "Let go!" then, "*Freeze!*" the children let go of the parachute and stand "frozen" in place while the parachute falls down on them.

SPECIFIC GOAL:
1. *Cooperative play*
2. *Tactile stimulation*
3. *Large motor activity*

SUGGESTIONS and VARIATIONS:
1. This activity should be preceded by MUSHROOM (p. 59).

BUMPS

SET UP and MATERIALS:
1. Parachute in available indoor or outdoor space.

PROCEDURE:
1. Position children at seams of the parachute standing up holding the parachute with the claw hold grip.
2. At the *teacher's* direction, "Lift!" children lift parachute *walk* forward two steps and quickly sit down in *ready position.*
3. The parachute will float down and settle on their heads and bodies (children just love this!).
4. As children look underneath at one another, they all seem to resemble BUMPS in the parachute.

SPECIFIC GOAL:
1. *Tactile stimulation*
2. *Cooperative play*

SUGGESTIONS and VARIATIONS:
1. Children also enjoy extending their arms overhead to shape the parachute like a canopy. They can see one another better in this situation.

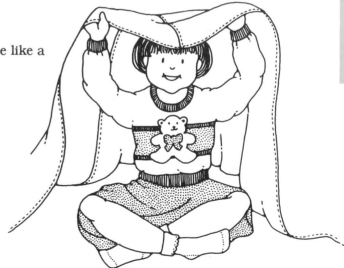

61

MAKE A TENT

SET UP and MATERIALS:
1. Parachute in available indoor or outdoor space.

PROCEDURE:
1. Position children at seams of parachute standing up holding the parachute with the claw hold grip.
2. At the *teacher's* direction, "Lift!" the children lift the parachute, *walk* forward one step while pulling the parachute behind them and sitting down on the edge of the parachute. By sitting down inside the parachute they seal in as much air as possible.
3. All participants are inside of the parachute while the parachute is in the shape of a dome tent.

SPECIFIC GOAL:
1. *Directionality*
2. *Cooperative play*
3. *Imagery*

SUGGESTIONS and VARIATIONS:
1. Spectators outside of the parachute enjoy seeing the dome tent take shape. Try to provide opportunities for children to be spectators so that they can see this neat shape.

FIND THE GHOSTS

SET UP and MATERIALS:
1. Parachute in available indoor or outdoor space.

PROCEDURE:
1. Position children at the seams of the parachute standing up and holding the parachute with the claw hold grip.
2. At the *teacher's* direction, "Lift!" the children lift the parachute. Then, the *teacher* says *Freeze!* and the children immediately release the parachute but keep their arms extended overhead.
3. The parachute will settle down, usually covering part of the group. These are the GHOSTS we have found.
4. The *teacher* should invite and initiate conversation with these GHOSTS.

SPECIFIC GOAL:
1. *Cooperative play*
2. Language experience
3. *Imagery*

SUGGESTIONS and VARIATIONS:
1. The parachute must be released simultaneously by everyone.
2. No one should pull or yank the parachute towards them as they *freeze* and release. The *teacher* must guide the correct execution of these directions.

PARACHUTE

63

VOLCANO

SET UP and MATERIALS:
1.   Parachute in available indoor or outdoor space.

PROCEDURE:
1.   Position the children at the seams of the parachute standing up and holding the parachute with the claw hold grip.
2.   At the *teacher's* direction, "Lift!" the children lift the parachute (using straight arms) up and over their heads.
3.   At the *teacher's* direction, VOLCANO! the children quickly squat down and pull the edge of the inflated parachute to the ground. The children are outside of the parachute and the air that is trapped inside of the parachute makes it look like a VOLCANO.
4.   Repeat frequently as children enjoy this activity.

SPECIFIC GOAL:
1.   *Cooperative play*
2.   *Imagery*

SUGGESTIONS and VARIATIONS:
1.   Instead of squatting, have children kneel on the edge of the inflated parachute to seal the air in. Then encourage them to lay on their stomach's and do the ALLIGATOR CRAWL (p. 125) toward the center aperture to make the VOLCANO erupt!

TAKE A WALK

SET UP and MATERIALS:
1. Parachute in available indoor or outdoor space.

PROCEDURE:
1. Position children at seams of the parachute standing up and holding the parachute with the claw hold grip.
2. The *teacher* directs the children to hold the parachute with their right hand while putting their left hand on their waist. When everyone is ready, then, the group will "TAKE the parachute for A WALK." The children will travel all the way around until they return to their "home." This "home" is their starting spot.
3. Repeat this activity. Children now hold the parachute with their left hand and they place their right hand on their waist.

SPECIFIC GOAL:
1. *Locomotor transport skills*
2. *Laterality*
3. *Directionality*
4. *Cooperative play*

SUGGESTIONS and VARIATIONS:
1. Other possible modes of travel:
   a. *Jump*
   b. *Jog*
   c. *Skip*
   d. *Tiptoe*
2. This activity is especially effective when accompanied by music.

PARACHUTE

65

COLOR SHAKE

SET UP and MATERIALS:
1. Parachute in available indoor or outdoor space.
2. Nerf balls of the same size but in a variety of colors placed on top of the parachute.

PROCEDURE:
1. Position children at seams of parachute standing up and holding the parachute with the claw hold grip.
2. Have children "count off" by naming the colors of the nerf balls on the parachute in turn, i.e. yellow, orange, green (then repeating the color sequence, yellow, orange, green).
3. Direct children to SHAKE THE PARACHUTE to see which color will remain after two minutes of shaking.
4. Two minutes is the longest you should go before stopping for a rest. Arm muscles ache easily with vigorous SHAKING OF THE PARACHUTE.

SPECIFIC GOAL:
1. *Cooperative play*
2. *Visual discrimination*
3. *Eye tracking*

SUGGESTIONS and VARIATIONS:
1. With young children, or as an initial experience, the entire group might just try to shake out one color. This eliminates the need to have children "count off" by color.

FRUIT SALAD

SET UP and MATERIALS:
1. Parachute in available indoor or outdoor space
2. Nerf balls of various colors
3. Sponge

PROCEDURE:
1. Position children at seams of parachute standing up holding the parachute with the claw hold grip.
2. As the *teacher* tosses in the balls, the balls are identified with the names of fruits (i.e. red would be cherries).
3. Encourage the children to "mix the FRUIT SALAD" by shaking and tossing the nerf balls while the parachute is being vigorously shaken up and down.
4. Then, the *teacher* tosses in a sponge saying, "What! oh dear, my kitchen sponge is in there. We don't want my kitchen sponge in our delicious FRUIT SALAD. Let's try to shake out that sponge." The *teacher* continues the dialogue by saying, "Let's try not to lose any of our yummy fruit, though."
5. Children cooperate and try to shake out only the sponge.

SPECIFIC GOAL:
1. *Cooperative play*
2. *Visual discrimination*
3. *Eye tracking*

SUGGESTIONS and VARIATIONS:
1. COLOR SHAKE (p. 66) is a wonderful accompanying activity.

PARACHUTE

POP, POP, POPCORN POP

SET UP and MATERIALS:
1. Parachute in available indoor or outdoor space.
2. Nerf balls (at least three)

PROCEDURE:
1. Position the children at the seams of the parachute standing up and holding the parachute with the claw hold grip.
2. The *teacher* explains to the children that the parachute is now a pan for POPping POPCORN. The children pretend to "pour in the oil!" and as the *teacher* directs, the children take a step backwards (parachute surface tightens and stretches as "the pan is heating up.") The children are also directed to tighten their grip and the *teacher* tosses in at least three nerf balls (explaining that we shall pretend these are kernels of popcorn).
3. At the *teacher's* command, "Shake!" all of the children vigorously SHAKE THE PARACHUTE up and down POPping the POPCORN. The group should be encouraged to cooperate and keep the popcorn in the pan.

SPECIFIC GOAL:
1. *Cooperative play*
2. *Directionality*
3. *Imagery*

SUGGESTIONS and VARIATIONS:
1. The initial experience should last no longer than two minutes. Arm muscles tend to ache after an experience of vigorous shaking. It's best to rest, try another activity, then return to POP, POP, POPCORN, POP.
2. Great laughter ensues if a "hole" is found in the pan where the popcorn escapes. Always return the "popcorn" to the "pan" and continue to shake. It might be wise to assign specific children to retrieve the "missing kernels."

YING AND YANG BALL SHAKE

SET UP and MATERIALS:
1. Parachute in available indoor or outdoor space.
2. Assorted medium size nerf balls placed in the middle of the parachute. Suggested minimum number is five.

PROCEDURE:
1. Position the children at the seams of the parachute standing and holding the parachute with the claw hold grip.
2. At the midway point of the parachute, divide the players into two groups designating one half as YING and the other half as YANG. These are the two groups.
3. The goal of this game is to SHAKE THE PARACHUTE and have the fewest number of balls land on your group's side of the floor. The children will need to cooperate to keep the balls in the parachute as the nerf balls come close to their edge.

SPECIFIC GOAL:
1. *Cooperative play*
2. *Directionality*

SUGGESTIONS and VARIATIONS:

PARACHUTE

SHADOW SHOOT

SET UP and MATERIALS:
1. Parachute in available indoor or outdoor space.
2. Six five inch or larger nerf balls

PROCEDURE:
1. Position the children at the seams of the parachute standing and holding the parachute with the claw hold grip.
2. The *teacher* tosses into the center of the parachute the nerf balls (minimum number of six).
3. Ask three children to let go of the parachute. These three children will *walk* underneath the inflated parachute as the *teacher* says, "*Walk!*"
4. Other children will follow the *teacher's* direction to "Shake!"
5. The *teacher* should give the command, "*Walk!*" directly after instructing the group to "Shake!"
6. The children under the parachute attempt to shoot the balls off of the parachute. When there are no more balls left, the game continues when three new children are chosen.

SPECIFIC GOAL:
1. *Visual discrimination*
2. *Cooperative play*

SUGGESTIONS and VARIATIONS:
1. The SHADOWS of the balls assist the children under the parachute to locate them and to SHOOT them off of the parachute.

70

EXCHANGE PLACES

SET UP and MATERIALS:
1. Parachute in available indoor or outdoor space

PROCEDURE:
1. Position children at the seams of the parachute standing up and holding the parachute with the claw hold grip.
2. Ask two children across from each other to let go of the parachute. These two children will exchange places, *walking* beneath the inflated parachute at the *teacher's* command, "*Walk!*"
3. Other children will follow the *teacher's* directions to:
    a. "Touch the parachute to toes"
    b. "Lift" (means with straight arms the children will lift parachute up and over their heads). This is an important direction.
4. The *teacher* should give command, "*Walk!*" immediately after saying "Lift."
5. The *teacher* says, "Down to your waist," just as the two children exchanging places come close to reaching their new destinations.
6. Before choosing two new players to EXCHANGE PLACES, ask everyone to check to see if they are standing at the seams of the parachute and holding it with the claw hold grip (after rolling the edge three times).

SPECIFIC GOAL:
1. *Directionality*
2. *Spatial awareness*
3. *Cooperative play*

SUGGESTIONS and VARIATIONS:
1. This is a wonderful activity for every participant to have a chance to EXCHANGE PLACES.
2. Have two to four children drop the parachute at one time to EXCHANGE PLACES on the *teacher's* command, "*Walk!*" Direct children in this situation to "find a new place."
3. Encourage the players not to "bump into one another" while under the parachute.

71

DOORBELL

SET UP and MATERIALS:
1. Parachute in available indoor or outdoor space.
2. Children are barefoot (if indoors).

PROCEDURE:
1. Position children at the seams of the parachute sitting at *ready position.* Then, ask them to lay down on their backs under the parachute with the parachute covering up to their necks. Remind them to keep their arms and hands covered.
2. The *teacher* selects a "door person" to sit down on the aperture (center hole of the parachute) with eyes closed and head down. The *teacher* slips the bell into the hands of one of the children who is laying down.
3. The *teacher* asks the "door person" to open his eyes and to listen for the bell to be rung. The "door person" tries to guess who is ringing the DOORBELL.
4. This game continues with a new "door person" selected and the bell being given to a new player.

SPECIFIC GOAL:
1. *Auditory discrimination*
2. *Cooperative play*

SUGGESTIONS and VARIATIONS:

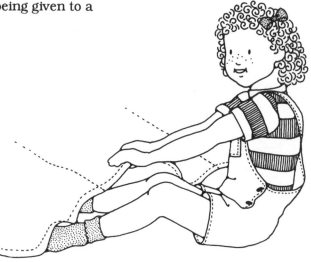

FAST FOOD GAME

SET UP and MATERIALS:
1. Parachute in available indoor or outdoor space.

PROCEDURE:
1. Position children sitting down in *ready position* at the seams of the parachute using the claw hold grip.
2. The *teacher* helps the children count off by saying, "Hamburger," "Hot Dogs," "French Fries," "Milkshakes." The sequence is repeated so each child has an identification. In turn, each person is asked to say aloud their identification.
3. The *teacher* then calls out one of the four FAST FOODS, either, "Hamburger," "Hot Dog," "French Fries," Milkshakes." The children with that identification, release the parachute and take a step in underneath the parachute to perform a simple stunt or trick (such as turning around, doing a jumping jack, touching toes, clapping hands, etc...). Then, they quickly return to their spot and grab the edge of the parachute before it touches the ground.
5. The *teacher* can call out more than one FAST FOOD at a time.

SPECIFIC GOAL:
1. *Locomotor skills*
2. *Directionality*
3. *Cooperative play*

SUGGESTIONS and VARIATIONS:
1. With younger children the *teacher* should have only two FAST FOODS "counted off" such as "Hamburger" or "Hot Dog."
2. Also, with younger children, the *teacher* should be very specific as to the stunt or trick. The *teacher* should say, "Clap your hands." Then, the group could progress during other turns to do a stunt of their choice.

EYES, EARS, NOSE, CHIN

SET UP and MATERIALS:
1. Parachute in available indoor or outdoor space.

PROCEDURE:
1. Position children standing at the seams of the parachute using the claw hold grip.
2. Children count off by saying, EYES, EARS, NOSE, CHIN. Sequence is repeated until all the children have been given the identification of a facial part. This is their group.
3. The *teacher* says, "Touch the parachute to toes, ready lift." The *teacher* then calls out either,
   a. *Walk* EYES or
   b. *Walk* EARS or
   c. *Walk* NOSE or
   d. *Walk* CHIN
4. The children with that identification release the parachute *and walk* (stress *walk*) to the spot recently vacated by another member of that team. Therefore, those children whose facial part was called are now standing in a new spot.

SPECIFIC GOAL:
1. *Locomotor skills*
2. *Directionality*
3. *Cooperative play*

SUGGESTIONS and VARIATIONS:
1. Children find it very amusing to hear the *teacher* say, *Walk* NOSE etc... But this is your way of managing the group so that they do not bump into one another.
2. With an older group you could say, *Jog* NOSE or *Skip* NOSE if you feel there is enough locomotor control and accidents will not occur as children move quickly to their new spot. It is always best to start them moving slowly until they are familiar with the activity.

PASS THE PARACHUTE

SET UP and MATERIALS:
1. Parachute in available indoor or outdoor space.

PROCEDURE:
1. Position the children at the seams of the parachute standing up and holding the parachute with the claw hold grip.
2. Go around to each child in a clockwise rotation and identify who they are passing the parachute to.
3. Direct the children to *freeze* their feet so that just their hands will open and PASS THE PARACHUTE in a clockwise direction.

SPECIFIC GOAL:
1. *Directionality*
2. *Cooperative play*
3. *Dexterity*

SUGGESTIONS and VARIATIONS:
1. With older children include challenges such as PASSing THE PARACHUTE to the right or left, PASS THE PARACHUTE fast or slow, and changing the instruction without the parachute coming to a complete stop.

PARACHUTE

ABC'S AND 123'S

SET UP and MATERIALS:
1.   Parachute in available indoor or outdoor space.

PROCEDURE:
1.   Position children sitting down in *ready position* at the seams of the parachute using the claw hold grip.
2.   One child can demonstrate by moving around the outside of the parachute (behind the backs of the sitting players) and returning to his "spot" (the point at which he started).
3.   The *teacher* helps children count off by saying, A, B, C,1, 2, 3. The sequence is repeated until each child has an identification. In turn, the *teacher* asks everyone to say aloud their identification.
4.   The group is asked to stand up. The *teacher* says, "Touch the parachute to your toes, ready, lift."
5.   The *teacher* then calls out one of the six identifications, either, A, B, C, 1, 2, 3. The children with that identification release the parachute and *walk* around the outside of the parachute returning to their original "spot."
6.   Play continues following the same procedure with the *teacher* calling another identification.

SPECIFIC GOAL:
1.   *Locomotor transport skills*
2.   *Spatial orientation*
3.   *Cooperative play*

SUGGESTIONS and VARIATIONS:
1.   Children can be asked to use other *locomotor movements* such as:
      a. *Gallop*
      b. *Jump*
      c. *Skip*
      d. *March*
      e. On *tiptoes*
      f. Different animal walks (pp. 125 - 134).
2.   The *teacher* can challenge the children to return to their "spot" before the center of the parachute touches the floor.

CAT AND MOUSE

SET UP and MATERIALS:
1. Parachute on indoor matted or carpeted area
2. Or parachute outdoors on grass

PROCEDURE:
1. Position children at seams of the parachute sitting at *ready position* with their shoes off (whether indoors or outdoors).
2. Designate one child to be the "mouse."   The "mouse" is to do the ALLIGATOR CRAWL (p.125) while under the parachute.
3. Another child is chosen to be the "cat." The "cat" CREEPS (p.126) on top of the parachute.
4. Everyone else SHAKES THE PARACHUTE up and down while holding onto the parachute with the claw hold grip.
5. The "cat" is to capture the "mouse" by touching the "mouse" on the back.
6. The activity continues with a new "mouse" and a new "cat."

SPECIFIC GOAL:
1. *Cross lateral* movement with the ALLIGATOR CRAWL and with the CREEP.
2. *Visual discrimination*
3. *Cooperative play*
4. *Large motor activity*

SUGGESTIONS and VARIATIONS:
1. With a transparent parachute, the "mouse" would be easily visible. Therefore, the *teacher* should remind the "mouse" to ALLIGATOR CRAWL quickly to avoid detection.

PARACHUTE

77

BALL ROLL

SET UP and MATERIALS:
1. Parachute in available indoor or outdoor space
2. Seven inch diameter rubber utility ball

PROCEDURE:
1. Position the children at the seams of parachute standing and holding with the claw hold grip.
2. In a cooperative manner, children will attempt to roll the ball around the perimeter of the parachute without interruption.
3. Children should be alert and ready to assist in guiding the ball smoothly as it travels on the perimeter of the parachute.
4. The ball will not move if the parachute is a taut smooth surface. Children must cooperate to lift and lower the parachute when it is appropriate.

SPECIFIC GOAL:
1. *Laterality*
2. *Directionality*
3. *Cooperative play*

SUGGESTIONS and VARIATIONS:

PARTNERS TOUCH

SET UP and MATERIALS:
1. Parachute in available indoor or outdoor space.

PROCEDURE:
1. Children stand at the seams of the parachute holding it with the claw hold grip.
2. The *teacher* determines how many children are in the group and divides the group so that two children have the same number when they "count off."
3. The *teacher* gives commands: example - "Number 6, hand to hand."
4. The two children with that number must quickly drop the parachute, go under the parachute to follow the *teacher's* instructions, then return to their original spots before the parachute touches down.
5. The *teacher* must also give the command, "Lift!" so that the rest of the group knows to lift the parachute and keep it up until the *teacher* says, "Down to your waist."

SPECIFIC GOAL:
1. *Auditory memory*
2. *Body image awareness*
3. *Cooperative play*

SUGGESTIONS and VARIATIONS:
1. Make sure every child knows his or her number.
2. The *teacher* can call out two numbers so that four children can participate. But partners still touch partners.
3. Some suggestions:
   a. "Ear to Ear"
   b. "Head to Head"
   c. "Nose to Nose"
   d. "Side to Side"
   e. "Bottom to Bottom"
   f. "Toes to Toes'
   g. "Cheek to Cheek"
   h. "Thumb to Thumb"
   i. "Elbow to Elbow"
   j. "Ankle to Ankle"
   k. "Knee to Knee"
   l. "Hip to Hip"
   m. "Wrist to Wrist"
   n. "Tummy to Tummy"

WHOOZ MISSING

SET UP and MATERIALS:
1.   Parachute in available indoor or outdoor space.

PROCEDURE:
1.   Children sit at the seams of the parachute in *ready position*. They hold the parachute with the claw hold grip.
2.   The *teacher* designates the first "detective." The "detective" sits on the aperture of the parachute. The "detective" has his head bent and covers his eyes with his hand.
3.   The *teacher* selects the first "Whooz." The "Whooz" slips under the parachute moving around under the parachute using either the ALLIGATOR CRAWL (p. 125) or the CREEPing movement (p.126).
4.   When "Whooz" has begun to move, the "detective" uncovers his eyes and tries to use visual clues to figure out WHOOZ MISSING. The "detective" remains sitting on the aperture of the parachute while guessing the identity of "Whooz."
5.   Other children are vigorously SHAKING THE PARACHUTE up and down because this distraction adds more of a challenge for the "detective."
6.   The "detective" selects a replacement and "Whooz" selects a replacement too. The game resumes with these two new players.

SPECIFIC GOAL:
1.   *Visual memory*
2.   *Cooperative play*

SUGGESTIONS and VARIATIONS:
1.   Establish a short but reasonable "guessing time."
2.   It is a good idea to refer to ALLIGATOR CRAWL (p. 125) and CREEP (p. 126) for a review of these skills prior to the start of WHOOZ MISSING.

STORY OF THE STORM

SET UP and MATERIALS:
1. Parachute in available indoor or outdoor space.

PROCEDURE:
1. Position children at the seams of the parachute sitting at *ready position* holding the parachute with the claw hold grip.
2. The *teacher* gives the following narrative:
"Look at this parachute. Let's make it nice and smooth just like the water on a lake. Sometimes, the wind blows over the lake and small ripples and waves begin. How gently can we make these small ripples and waves with this parachute? (Continuing with expression and excitement), the *teacher* says, "Do you feel the wind starting to get stronger? Let's make bigger and faster moving waves since the wind is blowing harder. Oh! Oh! Here comes the rain! It is a big storm. Can we SHAKE THE PARACHUTE so that it sounds like the waves on the water?" (Slowing down the pace of the narrative), the *teacher* says in a quiet voice, "The rain is starting to slow down. Let's slow down our shaking. The rain has stopped. The waves are gentle once more. We can make our parachute lake look nice and calm again."

SPECIFIC GOAL:
1. *Cooperative play*
2. *Laterality*
3. *Directionality*
4. *Imagery*

SUGGESTIONS and VARIATIONS:

PARACHUTE CATCH

SET UP and MATERIALS:
1. Parachute in available indoor or outdoor space.

PROCEDURE:
1. Position children at seams of parachute standing and holding the parachute with the claw hold grip.
2. The *teacher* reminds children that for this activity, the group needs to stand still. The *teacher* can say, "*freeze* your feet."
3. At the *teacher's* direction, "Lift!" the children lift the parachute and release it on the command, "Let go!" The *teacher*, then, immediately gives the direction, "Catch!" The children try to catch the parachute before it floats to the ground.
4. After a few practices, the *teacher* can pause before giving the command, "Catch!"

SPECIFIC GOAL:
1. *Directionality*
2. *Listening skills*
3. *Cooperative play*
4. *Dexterity*

SUGGESTIONS and VARIATIONS:
1. After giving the command, "Let go!" the *teacher* can say, "Kneel down!" Then, the *teacher* can say, "Catch!"
2. Remind children that "kneeling" means to be on ones knees and keeping their backs straight.

TAKE IT IF YOU CAN

SET UP and MATERIALS:
1. Parachute in available indoor or outdoor space.
2. Bean bag

PROCEDURE:

1. Position the children at the seams of the parachute standing up and holding the parachute with the claw hold grip.
2. So that two children are assigned the same number, follow this procedure: if there are ten children, the *teacher* helps children count off by saying one, two, three, four, five. Thus, children with the same number are standing opposite each other. The number that represents one half the number of children in the group is the highest number in the count off sequence.
3. The bean bag is placed on the floor under the center or aperture of the parachute.
4. The *teacher* tells the children to touch the parachute to their toes, "Lift!" (using straight arms) the parachute up and over their heads.
5. Just after saying, "Lift!" the *teacher* calls out a number so those two children with that assigned number will *run* under the parachute. Both children attempt to be the first one to pick up the bean bag and to return to his or her original spot. He is chased by the other child with the same number but the person returning to the bean bag bearer's spot first is the winner.
6. The winner returns the bean bag to its location and the game continues with the *teacher* calling out another number.

SPECIFIC GOAL:
1. *Auditory memory*
2. *Spatial awareness*
3. *Directionality*

SUGGESTIONS and VARIATIONS:
1. This game is recommended for older children.
2. Body contact is avoided because the two children are racing for a specific spot rather than trying to tag another person.

83

PULL AND RELAX

SET UP and MATERIALS:
1. Parachute in indoor or outdoor space.

PROCEDURE:
1. Position the children at the seams of the parachute standing up and holding the parachute with the claw hold grip.
2. Direct the children to release one hand from the parachute and to turn their backs to the parachute.
3. Now, with their backs to the parachute, ask the children to grip the parachute again with both hands.
4. The *teacher* will say, PULL! and the children should place one foot forward to stretch the parachute (bent knees help).
5. On command from the *teacher*, RELAX! the children position their feet together.
6. Repeat this activity using the other foot.

SPECIFIC GOAL:
1. Exercise *upper body strength*
2. *Directionality*
3. *Cooperative play*

SUGGESTIONS and VARIATIONS:
1. For younger children the *teacher* does not have them turn their backs (ignore directions #2 and #3). Do ask the children to keep their feet together and while not moving, the children should PULL AND RELAX.

BIG GULP

SET UP and MATERIALS:
1.   Parachute in available indoor or outdoor space

PROCEDURE:
1.   Position children at the seams of the parachute sitting in *ready position.*
2.   Explain that this is a pretend game. The *teacher* begins by saying, "The parachute is hungry and we look very tasty as we sit around it."
3.   The *teacher* gives the following narrative as the parachute is slowly drawn up to cover the appropriate body parts. Children will need to begin by extending their legs under the parachute as this dialogue starts:
>   "As we start this feast,
>   The first thing that goes
>   Are my tasty toes.
>   Now, if you please
>   Gobble up these knees.
>   Yummy, Yummy,
>   It's up to my tummy.
>   Next to go in,
>   Is my tasty delicious chin.
>   Then, you know what it said
>   As it ate my head?
>   GULP!"

SPECIFIC GOAL:
1.   *Body image awareness*
2.   *Imagery*

SUGGESTIONS and VARIATIONS:
1.   GOOD NIGHT (p. 86) is an excellent follow up to this activity.

85

GOOD NIGHT

SET UP and MATERIALS:
1. Parachute in available indoor or outdoor space

PROCEDURE:
1. Position children at seams of parachute sitting in *ready position*. Then, ask them to lay down on their backs.
2. The *teacher* directs the children to "Pull the parachute up and over your face." The children can look through the material to observe the lights, etc... Encourage spontaneous feedback from the children of their observations.
3. Ask the children to be quiet and to listen to the sounds in the room and in the environment.

SPECIFIC GOAL:
1. *Auditory discrimination*
2. *Visual discrimination*
3. *Cooperative play*

SUGGESTIONS and VARIATIONS:
1. This is a wonderful quiet and calming close to any parachute activity.

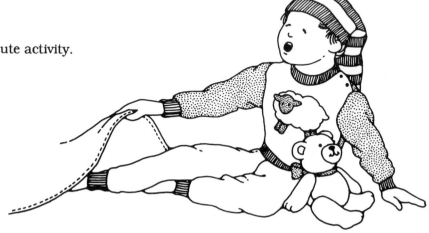

CLOSING PARACHUTE LESSON

SET UP and MATERIALS:
1. Parachute in available indoor or outdoor space

PROCEDURE:
1. Position children at seams of parachute standing up holding parachute with the claw hold grip.
2. The *teacher* directs children to stand with their feet shoulder width apart, their feet "frozen" in place.
3. Next, the *teacher* instructs the group to roll the parachute until they are told to stop. Arms will be outstretched and extended as they follow this instruction. It is important that the feet remain "frozen" in place.
4. The *teacher* tells the children, "Take one step in!" After taking that one step in, the group will again *freeze* their feet and continue to roll up the parachute. This sequence of rolling, stop, taking one step in etc... is continued until the parachute is about one half its original size.
5. At this time, the *teacher* directs the children to gently release the parachute as they set it down on the floor.
6. The class should step back and observe and comment on the parachute's appearance.

SPECIFIC GOAL:
1. Preparing the parachute for storage
2. *Cooperative play*
3. *Imagery*

SUGGESTIONS and VARIATIONS:
1. Some typical responses: "The parachute looks like a spider web." "It looks like a pancake." "I see the shape of a cloud."
2. This is another good language experience.

PARACHUTE

CHAPTER THREE
SIMPLE EQUIPMENT PLAY

EQUIPMENT

TITLES OF SIMPLE EQUIPMENT PLAY FOUND IN CHAPTER THREE

(Listed alphabetically with corresponding page number)

INTRODUCTION TO BALL PLAY

Children have an early fascination with balls. Babies grasp balls and toddlers run and follow after them. The ideas in this section will help you to further explore the possibilities and enhance any child's enjoyment with balls.

Because we emphasize exposure rather than proficiency, it is best if each child had his own ball. Balls need not be expensive. The size is much more important than the quality. We have found that seven inch balls are a universally appealing size for youngsters.

GAMES TO USE AS A FOLLOW UP AFTER WORKING WITH THIS CHAPTER:

- •FROGS AND FLIES (p. 30)
- •GHOST GUARD (p.16)
- •NAME BALL (p.16)
- •NO NAME BALL GAME (p.18)
- •"NO, THANK YOU!" BALL (p. 26)
- •OVER AND UNDER (p. 27)
- •PASS 'N COUNT (p. 29)

EQUIPMENT

MOVEMENT EXPLORATION WITH BODY PARTS

SET UP and MATERIALS:
1. A ball for each child
2. Available indoor or outdoor space
3. Children stand and hold their ball at their stomach. Children are separated to provide adequate *personal space* for each child during the entire lesson.

PROCEDURE:
Basic to all these suggestions is that the ball remain in contact with the designated body part for at least ten seconds. The *teacher* gives these directions:
1. "With the ball, show me how you can touch your head. Keep your ball there until I name the next body part..." suggestions:

ear	foot	wrist	shoulder	stomach
chest	thumb	neck	hip	chin
knee	elbow	nose	back	

2. "Put your ball on the floor and keep it from *rolling* away by using your..." (use the above suggestions)
3. "*Roll* the ball around your..." suggestions:
   ankle
   knee
   stomach
   hips
   head
   foot

SPECIFIC GOAL:
1. *Body image awareness*
2. *Dexterity*
3. *Small motor activity*

SUGGESTIONS:
1. For older children it is appropriate to include instructions for directions using right and left.
2. Laying on their backs, the children can hold their ball above certain body parts (this does get tiring so do it for a brief time).

BEGINNING BALL CATCHING

SET UP and MATERIALS:
1. Four to five children (maximum) standing in a row facing the *teacher*.
2. The *teacher* is facing the children and holding a ball.

PROCEDURE:
1. The *teacher* stands a foot away from the first child in the row. The *teacher* hands the ball to that child. The child returns the ball to the *teacher* in the same fashion.
2. The *teacher* proceeds to the next child and with each child in turn, this technique is repeated. The *teacher* is speaking in an encouraging manner to each child. Be sure to compliment the patience of those children awaiting their turn. Children can learn by watching one another.
3. The *teacher* increases the distance one to two feet as each round with the total row of children is completed. The children attempt to *catch* the ball with their hands and fingers. Trapping the ball against the body is only acceptable as part of the early experience. The ultimate goal, however, is to use only their hands and fingers to *catch* the ball when it is out in front of their bodies. The *teacher* should compliment and praise all such attempts.
4. The distance should be gradually increased to a maximum of six feet. The *teacher* needs to modify the goal according to the needs of the students, however.

SPECIFIC GOAL:
1. *Eye hand coordination*
2. *Dexterity*
3. *Small motor activity*

SUGGESTIONS and VARIATIONS:
1. Older children may work with a peer partner at this activity.

93

EQUIPMENT

BEGINNING BALL BOUNCING

SET UP and MATERIALS:
1. Four to five children (maximum) standing in a row facing the *teacher*.
2. The *teacher* faces the children and is holding a ball.
3. Four to five balls ready to distribute to the children after the demonstration.

PROCEDURE:
1. The *teacher* demonstrates the drop and *catch* of BALL BOUNCING. The child holds the sides of the ball with his fingertips; the child is standing with feet apart in a *straddle* position. The child drops the ball (does not push it down), bends his knees and recaptures the ball with his fingertips.
2. The *teacher* distributes a ball to each child. Children practice the drop and *catch* of BALL BOUNCING.
3. The *teacher* must monitor each child individually to reinforce the proper demonstrated technique. Remember to compliment and encourage all of the effort the children make with this skill.

SPECIFIC GOAL:
1. *Eye hand coordination*
2. *Dexterity*
3. *Small motor activity*

SUGGESTIONS and VARIATIONS:
1. With older children proceed to true bouncing by positioning the fingertips closer to the top of the ball while avoiding palm contact with the ball. Encourage them to use the fingertips to push the ball down in a true BALL BOUNCING fashion.

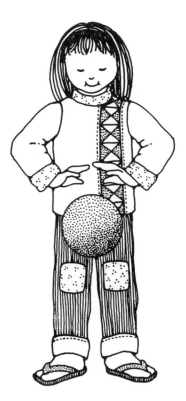

GROUND BALL

SET UP and MATERIALS:
1. Wall or backboard
2. A ball for every two children

PROCEDURE:
1. Distribution of balls should come after the demonstration by the *teacher*.
2. Position the children in pairs, six to eight feet away from the wall. Children are sitting in *ready position* as the *teacher* uses one pair of students for the demonstration.
3. Children stand together. Then, one child squats with the ball between his knees and with both hands *rolls* the ball toward the wall or backboard.
4. The partner waits and attempts to stop the ball just as soon as it touches the wall. The partner who stops the ball must not leave the partner's side until after the release of the ball. Partners should reverse jobs so that they each have a turn to *roll* the ball and to retrieve it on the rebound.
5. Play should continue until each child has had an opportunity to *roll* the ball at least a dozen times.

SPECIFIC GOAL:
1. *Eye hand coordination*
2. *Dexterity*
3. *Agility*
4. *Large and small motor activity*

SUGGESTIONS and VARIATIONS:
1. Older children should attempt to *roll* the ball with the one-step forward *cross lateral* movements releasing the ball in the "bowling fashion." This movement should be encouraged.

EQUIPMENT

BOWLING

SET UP and MATERIALS:
1. Children are divided into groups of five with a bowling pin and ball for each group.
2. Use a masking tape "X" on the spot where the pin should be located.
3. Adequate indoor space.

PROCEDURE:
1. Child should stand three to four feet away from the site of the pin.
2. With one child, demonstrate the straddle position and place the ball between the feet on the ground.
3. Give each child several turns *rolling* the ball over the tape mark without a bowling pin on it.
4. Now, place a bowling pin on the tape mark and give each child several chances until that child experiences success. The *teacher* should encourage the children to push the ball towards the pin with both hands.
5. As the child becomes more proficient, move the children back so that they are six to eight feet from the pin. Twelve feet is the maximum distance between a child and the bowling pin.

SPECIFIC GOAL:
1. *Eye hand coordination*
2. *Dexterity*
3. *Small motor activity*

SUGGESTIONS and VARIATIONS:
1. We have access to real bowling pins which are discards from the bowling alley. If you are unable to locate such a source, then get commercial ones which are usually made of plastic.
2. Ideally the pin should be about a foot away from a wall. The sound of the falling pin makes an authentic bowling alley noise.
3. Older children should be encouraged to perform a more authentic "side *roll*" of the ball instead of the straddle *roll* we described above.

INTRODUCTION TO ROPE PLAY

This section should give you ideas to use the rope for more than just *jumping*. The rope is an inexpensive piece of equipment that is adaptable for many purposes such as reinforcing language concepts or *tactile* learning. That is why most of the activities are especially suited for the children to be barefoot.

Each child should have a seven foot length rope. A flexible pliable rope is the best type and can be purchased at a hardware store in quantity. Ends of nylon ropes can be burned to prevent fraying and cotton ropes can be taped at each end.

All of the rope activities are planned for frequent review and repetition. For informational purposes a ROPE JUMPING lesson is included. However, our experiences have proven that it should not be introduced until the child is ready for this type of challenge and would not be frustrated by the experience.

EQUIPMENT

CIRCLES, TRIANGLES, AND SQUARES

SET UP and MATERIALS:
1. A rope for each child
2. Children are situated in sufficient space indoors or outdoors.

PROCEDURE:
Using the movement exploration approach: "Show me" or "Can you" the *teacher* asks each child to use the rope and to create a CIRCLE. After the completion of the three directions (#1,2,3) below, ask the children to form the TRIANGLE and repeat the three directions. These instructions should also be used with the shape of a SQUARE.

DIRECTIONS:
1. At the completion of the shape, the *teacher* leads a discussion regarding the special characteristics of that shape.
2. The *teacher* should now coordinate with a lesson on body parts. Ask the children to place in the shape their: foot, knee, elbow, hand, thumb, finger, ear, nose, bottom, etc... (avoid using left or right designation for young children).
3. Encourage children to use *locomotor skills* such as:
   a. "*Walk* on your circle"
   b. "*Jump* into your circle"
   c. "*Hop* around the circle"

SPECIFIC GOAL:
1. *Body image awareness*
2. *Locomotor skills*
3. *Spatial orientation*

SUGGESTIONS and VARIATIONS:
1. Use right and left designations with older children.
2. Place more than one body part in the shape.

STARTING PLAY WITH ROPES

SET UP and MATERIALS:
1. A rope for each child. Ropes are laying on the floor full length with adequate space between them to accommodate each child.
2. Children are barefoot (if indoors).

PROCEDURE:
This is material for several lessons. The *teacher* must judge how much to present to the children each time. The *teacher* leads each activity and encourages children to participate in the exploration.
1. "*Walking* very tall the length of the rope..."
   a. "*Walk* with your heel against your toe."
   b. "*Walk* backwards."
   c. "*Walk* sideways."
      • "*Walk* by crossing one foot in front of the other."
      • "You can step-together-step as you *walk*."
2. "Keeping the rope on the floor between your feet..."
   a. "Straddle *walk* forward."
   b. "Straddle *walk* backwards."
   c. "*Tiptoe* forward."
   d. "*Tiptoe* backwards."
   e. "*Jump* forward to the end of the rope, turn and return."
   f. "*Jump* forward to the end. Do not turn but still return."
3. Other movements:
   a. "*Jump* down to the end of your rope and back but with each *jump*, land on the opposite side of the rope."
   b. "*Hop* on the right foot to the end of the rope, but return by *hopping* on the left foot."
   c. "Perform, various animal walks down one side and then back. Examples: DOG WALK (p. 127), LAME DOG WALK (p.128), RABBIT JUMP (p. 129), FROG JUMP (p. 131).

SPECIFIC GOAL:
1. *Tactile* reinforcement
2. *Directionality*
3. *Balance*
4. *Locomotor transport skills*

SUGGESTIONS and VARIATIONS:
1. This material is well suited for review and repetition.

CONTINUING PLAY WITH ROPES

SET UP and MATERIALS:
1. A rope for each child. Ropes are laying on the floor in the shape of a circle. Adequate space is provided between the rope circles to provide each child an exploration area.
2. Children are barefoot (if indoors)

PROCEDURE:
1. As children get inside of a rope circle, encourage them to participate in all the exploration as the *teacher* says,
   a. "Stand very tall inside of the rope circle."
   b. "Make yourself very small inside the circle."
2. Continuing with the exploration, the *teacher* asks the children, "Stand very tall and *walk* heel against toe on the rope. Make several trips until you hear me say, 'Stop!'"
3. The *teacher* can ask the children to squat down low (they could put their hands on their waists to aid their *balance*) as they *walk* on the rope. They could make several trips travelling this way.
4. With one foot on the rope and one foot in the circle, ask the children to stand up very tall. They could *walk* keeping *balance.*
   a. Repeat with one foot on the rope and one foot outside of the circle. They should also have the chance to turn around and switch feet.
   b. Another variation is to do this on *tiptoes.*
5. With one foot in the circle and one foot outside of the circle (but not on the rope) children can straddle the rope and move around to different challenges.

SPECIFIC GOAL:
1. *Tactile* reinforcement
2. *Directionality*
3. *Balance*

SUGGESTIONS and VARIATIONS:
1. This material is well-suited for review and repetition.

100

HOME BODY

SET UP and MATERIALS:
1. A rope for each child. Ropes are laying on the floor in the shape of a circle.
2. Adequate space is provided between the rope circles to provide each child an exploration area.
3. Children are barefoot (if indoors).

PROCEDURE:
1. The *teacher* explains that the rope circle is the "home."
2. Ask the children to put their toes to the edge of the rope circle and to *jump* into their "home."
3. The children are then told to put their hands and feet in different "rooms of their home." Some suggestions:
   a. "Put one foot in the livingroom and the other foot in the kitchen."
   b. "Put one hand in the bedroom and one foot in the bathroom."
   c. "Put one foot in the garage and one hand in the laundry room."
4. The *teacher* can bring this game to a conclusion by telling the children, "Now, feet together, *jump* out of your front door!"

SPECIFIC GOAL:
1. *Balance*
2. *Locomotor skills*
3. *Tactile stimulation*

SUGGESTIONS and VARIATIONS:
1. As an additional closing activity, recite our version of a favorite nursery rhyme:
   "Jack be nimble, Jack be slick!
   Jack *jump* over your house real quick!"
2. After repeating the rhyme several times encourage the children to either *jump* or to *leap.*

101

EQUIPMENT

INNING AND OUTING

SET UP and MATERIALS:
1. A rope for each child. Ropes are laying on the floor in the shape of a circle. Adequate space is provided between rope circles to provide each child an exploration area.
2. Children are barefoot (if indoors).

PROCEDURE:
1. The *teacher* instructs the children to put their toes right up to the edge of the rope circle while standing outside of the circle.
2. (We have added right/left instructions for older children in parenthesis. It is developmentally inappropriate to expect preschool children to have *laterality* knowledge). The *teacher* directs the children to *jump*:
   Forward
   Backward
   Forward
   Forward
   Backward
   Backward
   Forward
   Sideways   (right)
   Sideways   (left)
   Sideways   (left)
   Sideways   (right)
   Forward
   Backward
   Backward

SPECIFIC GOAL:
1. *Balance*
2. *Locomotor transport skills*
3. *Directionality*
4. *Listening skills*

SUGGESTIONS and VARIATIONS:

102

KING COBRA

SET UP and MATERIALS:
1. A rope for each child.
2. Children are situated in sufficient indoor or outdoor space.
3. Children are barefoot (if indoors).

PROCEDURE:
1. The *teacher* instructs the children to place their ropes on the ground in the shape of a "snake." The "snakes" can all look different.
2. When the *teacher* says, "Go!" the children are to *walk* around without bumping into anyone and without stepping on any of the ropes. The ropes represent KING COBRA snakes.
3. The *teacher* adds variety by suggesting other locomotor skills:
   a. On *tiptoes*
   b. *Run*
   c. *Gallop*
   d. *Skip*
   e. *Hop*
   f. Go backwards around the "snakes"

SPECIFIC GOAL:
1. *Spatial awareness*
2. *Locomotor transport skills*

SUGGESTIONS and VARIATIONS:

103

ROPE JUMPING

SET UP and MATERIALS:
1. A rope for each child.
2. Adequate indoor or outdoor space is provided for each child to have sufficient space to explore.

PROCEDURE:
1. The *teacher* directs the children to hold both ends of the rope in their right hands. The *teacher* says: "Show me how you can turn the rope forward so the loop hits the ground next to your foot. Try keeping your arm down and use plenty of wrist action."
2. The *teacher* asks the children to attempt the same task as in #1 but this time each child should use his left hand.
3. After the children are comfortable with challenges #1 and #2, they should try the same tasks but now include *jumping*. As the loop hits the ground next to their feet, they should *jump*. This is done to allow practice for synchronization with the arms and legs.
4. The children should then hold the rope with both hands and JUMP ROPE back and forth under their feet (not over their head).
5. An attempt should be made to JUMP ROPE by turning the rope over the head and under the feet only when the child feels confident with the challenges already presented.

SPECIFIC GOAL:
1. *Balance*
2. *Laterality*
3. *Coordination*

SUGGESTIONS and VARIATIONS:
1. It is very important that prior to even considering this lesson the *teacher* should read INTRODUCTION TO ROPE PLAY (p. 97) at the beginning of this section.

INTRODUCTION TO BEAN BAGS

Bean bags are a wonderful source of *tactile stimulation*. Regardless of the fabric covering of the bean bag, the weight and texture are very pleasing. They are suitable to come before ball play for such challenges as tossing and *catching*. Bean bags are non-threatening and easy to hold.

We have found the best size for a bean bag is any square, rectangle or circle close to a four inch diameter.

GAMES TO USE AS A FOLLOW UP AFTER WORKING WITH THIS CHAPTER:

•MUSICAL BEAN BAGS (p. 33)
•"DOGGIE, DOGGIE, DROP YOUR BONE" (p. 28)
•SARDINES (p. 36)
•GEIGER COUNTER (p. 22)
•PIRATES OF THE CARIBBEAN (p. 31)

EQUIPMENT

MOVEMENT EXPLORATION WITH BODY PARTS

SET UP and MATERIALS:
1. A bean bag for each child.
2. Available indoor or outdoor space.
3. Children are sitting in *ready position* with the bean bag in front of them.

PROCEDURE:
1. It is very important that the bean bag stay in touch with the specific body part for at least ten seconds. The *teacher* gives directions and monitors the children to see how well they follow the challenge. The *teacher* should reinforce and praise generously.
1. The *teacher* says, "Keeping the bean bag in front of you on the floor, show me how you can touch your head to the bean bag. Keep your head on the bean bag until I name another body part..."

ear	stomach	nose
foot	chest	hip
wrist	thumb	chin
neck	shoulder	knee

2. Then, the children should be asked to pick up the bean bag and to touch various parts of the body with the bean bag.

SPECIFIC GOAL:
1. *Body image awareness*
2. *Tactile stimulation*
3. *Listening skills*

SUGGESTIONS and VARIATIONS:
1. For older children it is appropriate to include directions for right and left.
2. While laying on their backs, the children might try resting the bean bag on various body parts.

LOCOMOTOR ACTIVITIES

SET UP and MATERIALS:
1. A bean bag for each child.
2. Adequate indoor or outdoor space is provided for each child to have sufficient space to move freely.
3. Children are barefoot (if indoors).

PROCEDURE:
1. Children place their bean bag on the floor and follow the *teacher's* instructions. Remind the children to be ready:
   a. "With both feet together, *jump* over the bean bag..."
      (Repeat this series several times)
      (1)   Forward
      (2)   Backward
      (3)   Sideways
   b. "Without losing your *balance*, using just one foot, do *hop* overs." With older children, the *teacher* can indicate either the right foot or the left foot.
   c. "On all fours, please CREEP (p.126) around the bean bag..."
      (1)   Forward
      (2)   Backward (this is difficult)
   d. "We can try some animal walks around the bean bag."
      (1)   DOG WALK (p.127)
      (2)   LAME DOG WALK (p. 128)
      (3)   RABBIT JUMP (p. 129)
      (4)   INCH WORM (p. 130)
2. The children should place their bean bag on the floor and try to move it from one designated point to another using various parts of their body such as: head, elbows, feet, etc...
3. Holding the bean bag between their knees the children try:
   a. *Jumping* in place three times (increase repetition to ten times slowly)
   b. *Jumping* three steps forward (increase repetition to ten steps gradually)
   c. Sideways and backward *jumps* can also be attempted

SPECIFIC GOAL:
1. *Balance*
2. *Directionality*
3. *Locomotor transport skills*

SUGGESTIONS and VARIATIONS:

EQUIPMENT

BEGINNING BEAN BAG TOSS

SET UP and MATERIALS:
1. A dozen bean bags for each target.
2. A target on the wall or the floor.
3. Depending on the group size more than one target can be used.

PROCEDURE:
1. Child stands three to four feet from the target.
2. With one child, the *teacher* demonstrates how to pick up the bean bag with the favored hand to toss the bean bag at the target with an overhand *throw*. The overhand *throw* is grasping the bean bag in a fist, holding it near the ear (for example, "like scratching the ear"), then, releasing the bean bag with a forward push toward the target. The arm from the elbow to hand is moving toward the target.
3. The child gets as many chances to hit the target as there are bean bags.
4. As the children become more proficient, the children can move farther away from the target. We recommend a distance of six to eight feet (maximum).

SPECIFIC GOAL:
1. *Eye hand coordination*
2. *Directionality*
3. *Small motor activity*

SUGGESTIONS and VARIATIONS:
1. Targets can vary from a marked area on the wall or floor to a hoop on the wall or placed on the floor. The target should be a reasonable size to provide successful experiences.

108

FLIP THE PANCAKE

SET UP and MATERIALS:
1. A bean bag for each child
2. Children sit in *ready position*

PROCEDURE:
1. The *teacher* demonstrates by transferring the bag from one hand to another in quick movements. Children practice doing it themselves. The *teacher* stresses that it is important to watch the bean bag carefully and keep track of it. Once children have mastered #1, they can then proceed to #2.
2. When the children begin this activity, the *teacher* should encourage them to keep the bean bag as flat as possible. Sitting in *ready position* the children have both palms facing down with the thumbs touching side by side. Both hands are at about waist level in front of the stomach. Elbows are tucked in at the sides. The bean bag rests on the backs of their hands. On a signal from the *teacher*, both hands move so that the palms face up, little fingers are side by side and the bean bag has flipped into the palms of the hands. FLIP THE PANCAKE should continue for a maximum of five minutes.
3. Then, other variations can be attempted but, we recommend that all of these variations last for another five minute time period. Suggestions or variations to follow sitting in *ready position*:
    a. children kneel (keeping their backs straight)
    b. children stand
    c. children return to their knees and kneel
    d. children return to *ready position*

SPECIFIC GOAL:
1. *Eye hand coordination*
2. *Eye tracking*
3. *Small motor activity*

SUGGESTIONS and VARIATIONS:

109

STEPPING STONES

SET UP and MATERIALS:
1. At least two bean bags for each child.
2. Children sit in *ready position* against one wall facing the opposite wall which will be the other boundary.

PROCEDURE:
1. Sitting in *ready position* the children see the demonstration.
2. The *teacher* has one child demonstrate by placing his bean bags about six to eight inches apart on the floor. The *teacher* explains that the challenge is to move only by stepping on the bean bags which is why this activity is called STEPPING STONES.
3. At the direction "Start!", the children stand on the bean bags with one foot in front of the other. While *balancing* one foot on the front bean bag, each child will reach behind and pick up the back bean bag and place it six to eight inches in front so that the back foot can now take a step forward.
4. Children travel across the room by repeating this STEPPING STONE pattern. Once the children have reached the far wall or boundary they should return to *ready position* unless otherwise instructed by the *teacher*.

SPECIFIC GOAL:
1. *Balance*
2. *Directionality*
3. *Spatial Awareness*

SUGGESTIONS and VARIATIONS:
1. If you have three bean bags for each child, then, the children can easily mark their original starting points and return to it easily.
2. Encourage the children to place the bean bag no farther than the length of a normal step.
3. Moving sideways on the bean bags, the children can "step, together, step" or employ crossing the midline by "cross, step, cross."

INTRODUCTION TO HOOPS

Children feel a sense of security and familiarity when they are involved with a circle. It is usually the first shape that they recognize.

HOOPS and HOOP play inspire enthusiastic involvement. The HOOP can act as a space for movement participation. The HOOP also provides *tactile stimulation* and can be a wonderful source for imaginative play.

GAMES TO USE AS A FOLLOW UP AFTER WORKING WITH THIS CHAPTER:

•FRIENDLY MUSICAL HOOPS (p. 24)
•MERRY MUSICAL HOOPS (p. 25)
•JACK OR JILL RABBITS GO HOME (p. 21)

EQUIPMENT

EMPHASIZING BODY PARTS

SET UP and MATERIALS:
1. A hoop for each child
2. Available indoor or outdoor space
3. Children are sitting in *ready position* inside of their hoop.

PROCEDURE:
1. Children are first asked to put one body part inside of their hoop and to keep that body part in the hoop for a count of ten. This is necessary to reinforce body parts identification. Children should be frequently and generously praised as they attempt to follow these directions.
2. The *teacher* says, "Step out of your hoop. Show me how you can put into your hoop the body part that I name. Please leave that body part inside of your hoop until I name another body part..." Some suggestions:

ear	stomach	nose
foot	chest	hip
wrist	thumb	chin
neck	shoulder	knee

3. Children are then challenged to use their imagination and to follow these movement exploration type directions:
   a. "Put one part of your body inside the hoop..."
      (repeat with two, three, four, five body parts)
   b. "Standing inside of the hoop put one part of your body outside of the hoop..."
      (repeat with two, three, four, five body parts)

SPECIFIC GOAL:
1. *Body image awareness*
2. *Balance*

SUGGESTIONS and VARIATIONS:
1. For older children it is appropriate to include directions for right and left.

MOVEMENT EXPLORATION

SET UP and MATERIALS:
1. A hoop for each child. Hoops are placed on the floor with adequate space between them to accommodate each child.
2. Children are barefoot (if indoors).

PROCEDURE:
1. Children should place their toes at the rim of the hoop. The *teacher* instructs the children to put their feet together and get ready to *jump*. The right/left designations are meant only to be used with older children. The *teacher* says, "Get ready and *jump...*" (following this order)

    Forward
    Backward
    Forward
    Forward
    Backward
    Backward
    Forward
    Sideways   (right)
    Sideways   (left)
    Sideways   (left)
    Sideways   (right)
    Backwards

2. After following this pattern the children should straddle the hoop with one foot in the hoop and one foot out. The children can switch feet to change the foot which is inside the hoop and...
    a. Straddle *walk* forward
    b. Straddle *walk* backward
    c. *Tiptoe* forward
    d. *Tiptoe* backward

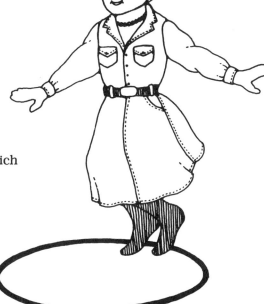

SPECIFIC GOAL:
1. *Tactile* reinforcement
2. *Directionality*
3. *Balance*

SUGGESTIONS and VARIATIONS:

113

STEERING WHEEL

SET UP and MATERIALS:
1. One hoop for each child.
2. Sufficient indoor or outdoor space for each child.
3. Children are sitting in *ready position* inside of their hoop.

PROCEDURE:
1. The *teacher* says, "Lift your hoop up to waist level using both hands. The hoop is your STEERING WHEEL. Turn it to the right or to the left using only your arms and shoulders."
2. The children are given enough time to practice before attempting the next challenge.
3. The children move their hoops so that they are holding the hoop in front of them. The *teacher* should repeat the instructions as was done in procedure #1. Children tire very easily with this activity so keep it as a short experience.

SPECIFIC GOAL:
1. *Directionality*
2. *Spatial orientation*
3. *Midline*
4. *Bilateral coordination*

SUGGESTIONS and VARIATIONS:
1. This is a good activity to use with the lesson HALOS. (p. 115)
2. For younger children do not concern yourself with saying left or right. The *teacher* should serve as a model so the children can just follow the action. This is an ideal opportunity for a fantasy activity such as "Let's take a trip..."

HALOS

SET UP and MATERIALS:
1. A hoop for each child.
2. Children are sitting in *ready position* inside of their hoop.
3. Available indoor or outdoor space.

PROCEDURE:
1. Discuss what a HALO is. The hoop is their HALO in this lesson.
2. The *teacher* says, "Raise the hoop over your head. Keep your arms straight. Try not to bend your elbows."
3. The *teacher* is encouraging and praising the efforts of the children. Then, the *teacher* says, "I will clap my hands; with that signal, release your hoop and let it fall down around your body."
4. Repeat the challenge several times. It can be varied by having children kneel or stand up instead of sitting in *ready position*.
5. Children really seem to enjoy the collective sound of all the hoops dropping together.

SPECIFIC GOAL:
1. *Spatial orientation*
2. *Directionality*
3. *Bilateral coordination*

SUGGESTIONS and VARIATIONS:
1. Encourage the children to drop the hoops without the hoops touching their bodies.
2. Older children can work with a partner and cooperatively execute the HALO and its release.

115

EGG BEATER

SET UP and MATERIALS:
1. One hoop for each child.
2. Sufficient indoor or outdoor space.

PROCEDURE:
1. The *teacher* demonstrates with one child. The *teacher* says, "Hold the hoop with your thumb and fingers. Stand the hoop on its edge in front of you."
2. At the *teacher's* direction, "Spin!" the child turns the hoop with a wrist action letting the hoop spin until it falls. The children wait for a signal from the *teacher* before retrieving their hoops.
3. Children enjoy making the hoop spin like an EGG BEATER. The group can pretend to be mixing up some tasty treats while using their EGG BEATERS.

SPECIFIC GOAL:
1. *Eye hand coordination*
2. *Eye tracking*
3. *Imagery*

SUGGESTIONS and VARIATIONS:
1. Older children enjoy the challenge of *jumping* in and out of the hoop before it comes to a stop. A more difficult challenge is to *hop* in and out of the hoop several times before it comes to a complete stop.

116

INTRODUCTION TO RHYTHM STICKS

RHYTHM STICKS (also known as Lumni Sticks) can be eight inches to twelve inches in length and about one half inch to one inch in thickness. They can be made from dowels purchased at a hardware or lumber store. However, commercially made rhythm sticks can be purchased in a variety of colors. Color adds a dimension and appeal to this piece of equipment.

RHYTHM STICKS provide good sensory and manipulative experiences. Any of the lessons included in this section are appropriate for centering or quieting the group. These are fine Circle Time activities.

MOVEMENT EXPLORATION WITH ONE STICK

SET UP and MATERIALS:
1. One rhythm stick for each child.
2. Children sitting in *ready position.*
3. Children put one hand behind their back.

PROCEDURE:
1. The *teacher* checks to see that each child begins by having his thumb on top of the stick. The stick is held straight up and down in a vertical position. On a signal from the *teacher*, the children move their fingers and thumb down the stick and then back up so that the thumb is on top again. Repeat this activity several times encouraging the children to gain speed while doing this exercise.
2. With this second activity, the children move their fingers and thumbs down the stick as they did before. But they stop at the midway point and twirl the stick. At a signal from the *teacher*, they stop the twirling and resume moving their fingers and thumb down to the bottom of the stick and then all the way back up to place the thumb on top again.

SPECIFIC GOAL:
1. *Directionality*
2. *Dexterity*
3. *Eye hand coordination*
4. *Small motor activity*

SUGGESTIONS and VARIATIONS:
1. Repeat these activities using the other hand.
2. When their thumb is on the top of the rhythm stick we tell the children, "This is putting the cap on!"

CROSSING THE MIDLINE

SET UP and MATERIALS:
1. One rhythm stick for each child.
2. Children sitting in *ready position.*

PROCEDURE:
1. Children grasp the stick in the middle holding it in the vertical position.
2. Each child will change the stick from one hand to his other hand keeping the stick within range of his eyesight.
3. The initial distance between hands should be just two inches to three inches so that it appears to be a hand off from one hand to the other.
4. Children do not increase the distance between their hands until they are comfortable and successful with the toss and *catch* motion. The maximum distance between hands should be twelve inches.
5. For all of this activity, the grasp must be kept in the middle of the vertically held stick.

SPECIFIC GOAL:
1. *Eye tracking*
2. *Eye hand coordination*
3. *Directionality*
4. *Midline*
5. *Small motor activity*

SUGGESTIONS and VARIATIONS:
1. CROSSING THE MIDLINE is considered an important reading readiness skill.
2. It is important for the *teacher* to frequently remind the children to keep their eyes on the rhythm stick.

KEEPING SEQUENCE

SET UP and MATERIALS:
1. Two rhythm sticks for each child.
2. Children are sitting in *ready position.*
3. The *teacher* holds two rhythm sticks to use in demonstration.

PROCEDURE:
1. Children will be told to repeat the pattern the *teacher* establishes. Performing the "tap tap" pattern, the child imitates the *teacher.* We find it best to initially give one child a turn, then we proceed to the next child.
2. Here are some successful two beat (or tap tap) patterns:
   a. tap tap quickly
   b. tap tap slowly
   c. tap tap loudly
   d. tap tap softly
3. Expand and increase beats, for example, tap tap pause tap.

SPECIFIC GOAL:
1. *Listening skills*
2. *Eye hand coordination*
3. *Auditory discrimination*
4. *Midline*

SUGGESTIONS and VARIATIONS:
1. For older children, the *teacher* can tap patterns with the rhythm sticks while the sticks are out of sight. Children must use only their listening abilities to repeat such a pattern.

TAP AND MARCH

SET UP and MATERIALS:
1. Two rhythm sticks for each child.
2. Children sitting in *ready position.*
3. The *teacher* holds two rhythm sticks ready to demonstrate.
4. Marching music either recorded or taped with appropriate machine.

PROCEDURE:
1. Allow about a minute for each experience, but with directions from the *teacher*, the children...
   a. "Tap sticks together."
   b. "Tap sticks up high with arms stretched up high."
   c. "Tap sticks down low."
   d. "Tap your sticks behind your back."
   e. "Tap your sticks on the ground."
2. With the children still seated, repeat the experiences of #1 while listening to the *marching* music.
3. Then, ask the children to stand up and *march* in place while the (a through e) experiences are repeated.
4. The *teacher* should initially lead, but it is fun to do these activities while *marching* throughout the space. Children enjoy taking turns being the TAP AND MARCH *leader.*

SPECIFIC GOAL:
1. *Locomotor skills*
2. *Coordination*
3. *Eye hand coordination*
4. *Midline*

SUGGESTIONS and VARIATIONS:
1. Encourage the children to move in good *marching* style with a lot of spirit and enthusiasm. The rhythm sticks add to the fun.

EQUIPMENT

121

INTRODUCTION TO MAT SKILLS

Opportunities to use mats and mat work should be provided frequently for every child. Preschool and young children are at an uninhibited age and willingly engage in all types of mat experiences.

It is crucial that skilled instruction be provided. It is at this stage that good habits and a wise regard for safety can be firmly ingrained.

Shoes and socks off is a must when working on mats. Removing shoes and socks provide *tactile stimulation* and benefit the *kinesthetic* with all activities. Repetition of experiences is highly beneficial. Each child should have several opportunities to do every MAT SKILL when the lessons are presented. The *teacher* should encourage and positively reinforce all of the efforts. Positive reinforcement and encouragement are a necessary accompaniment for all mat lessons.

An investment in quality mats should have the highest priority on your equipment list. Comparison shopping is advisable to locate the highest quality at the best price. We have found a five foot by twelve foot size with a one and one fourth inch to two inch thickness to be functional. Sometimes it will be necessary to use several of these mats at the same time. It is convenient to be able to attach the mats together.

The MAT SKILLS in this section are arranged in the sequence we feel they should be presented. This provides for progessional skills development.

GAMES TO USE AS A FOLLOW UP AFTER WORKING WITH THIS CHAPTER

•BODY DRILL (p. 15)
•HIT THE DECK (p. 38)
•ALLIGATORS IN THE SWAMP (p. 10)
•ANIMAL PARADE (p. 17)
•CATERPILLARS AND COCOONS (p. 43)

LOG ROLL

SET UP and MATERIALS:
1. Sufficient mat, rug, or grassy area to accommodate the entire group.
2. Children are barefoot (if indoors).

PROCEDURE:
1. The *teacher* guides each child to lie on his stomach (prone) on the mat with arms extended over his head, palms touching, legs together and straight.
2. The *teacher* explains that the "motor" to start the movement is located in the stomach and hips. When the "motor" starts, it will be important for the stomach and hips to help the child *roll* like a log.
3. It is very important for the *teacher* to encourage each child to slowly and carefully *turn* and *roll.* The *teacher* should also stress that the legs and arms must be kept as straight as possible.

SPECIFIC GOAL:
1. *Tactile stimulation*
2. *Body awareness*
3. *Agility*
4. *Vestibular stimulation*

SUGGESTIONS and VARIATIONS:
1. Crooked LOG ROLLING can be corrected when straight arms and straight legs are reestablished.

ALLIGATOR CRAWL

SET UP and MATERIALS:
1. Sufficient mat, rug, or grassy area to accommodate the entire group.
2. Children are barefoot (if indoors).

PROCEDURE:
1. Demonstrating at first with one child, the *teacher* has the child lie down prone (on his stomach). The *teacher* positions the child's limbs in this starting position:
   a. Right arm is extended forward
   b. Left knee is bent
   c. Right leg is straight
   d. Left arm is bent at the elbow and is placed near the waist
2. With the ALLIGATOR CRAWL, children are encouraged to move forward with the *cross lateral* pattern. The *teacher* should note any child who cannot sustain this *cross lateral* pattern movement.
3. It is very important for children to keep the trunk of their body in contact with the mat surface (or rug or grass) at all times. The *teacher* can say, "Remember to push your chest down!"

SPECIFIC GOAL:
1. *Cross laterality*
2. *Directionality*
3. *Vestibular stimulation*
4. *Tactile stimulation*

SUGGESTIONS and VARIATIONS:
1. For a child who cannot sustain the *cross lateral* movement the *teacher* should re-position the limbs and guide the child's movement.
2. Children seem to have the most difficulty keeping their knees bent. The *teacher* should be prepared to give verbal cues.

125

EQUIPMENT

CREEP

SET UP and MATERIALS:
1. Sufficient mat, rug, or grassy area to accommodate the entire group.
2. Children are barefoot (if indoors).

PROCEDURE:
1. Using one person for demonstration, the *teacher* explains with this movement it is necessary to, "Get down on all fours" (hands and knees).
2. After making sure that the child who is doing the demonstration is "down on all fours," the *teacher* guides the forward motion of the body by encouraging efficient cross patterning movement which means the right hand moves forward when the left knee moves forward, and the left hand moves forward when the right knee is moving forward.
3. The general population erroneously thinks that this is the way babies "crawl." More accurately, babies CREEP.

SPECIFIC GOAL:
1. *Locomotor skill*
2. *Cross lateral*
3. *Vestibular stimulation*
4. *Tactile stimulation*

SUGGESTIONS and VARIATIONS:
1. The backward CREEP is also an important movement.

126

DOG WALK

SET UP and MATERIALS:
1. Indoor area (covered by mats or rug) large enough to accommodate the group of children.
2. Children are barefoot (if indoors).

PROCEDURE:
1. The *teacher* tells the children, "Please *walk* and notice how your feet move with one foot in front of the other."
2. Continuing, the *teacher* says, "Now, return to your starting point. Then, place your hands (with palms down) on the mat. Bend your knees slightly." At this time, the *teacher* should check the position of each student.
3. Also the *teacher* should verify that each student's body weight is evenly distributed on the feet and hands.
4. Now the students are directed to establish the *walking* rhythm they noticed with direction #1. It helps to have a set path or route to follow from beginning to end.

SPECIFIC GOAL:
1. *Laterality*
2. *Coordination*
3. *Tactile stimulation*
4. *Kinesthetic awareness*
5. *Vestibular stimulation*
6. *Balance*

SUGGESTIONS:
1. Children should be encouraged to take their time. Maintaining body control is very important.

EQUIPMENT

LAME DOG WALK

SET UP and MATERIALS:
1. Indoor area (covered by mats or rug) large enough to accommodate the entire group of children.
2. Children are barefoot (if indoors).

PROCEDURE:
1. The *teacher* asks the children to demonstrate the DOG WALK (p. 127).
2. It is important that each child move only as fast as body control can be maintained while doing the DOG WALK or the LAME DOG WALK.
3. Children are asked to return to the starting point. They keep both hands on the mats or rug but use only one foot. This is the difference between the DOG WALK and the LAME DOG WALK.
4. By keeping both hands on the mats or rug, they will be resting most of their body weight on their hands and moving their foot in the *hopping* motion.
5. It helps to have a set path or route to follow from beginning to end.

SPECIFIC GOAL:
1. *Balance*
2. *Coordination*
3. *Kinesthetic awareness*
4. *Laterality*
5. *Tactile stimulation*
6. *Vestibular stimulation*

SUGGESTIONS and VARIATIONS:
1. Children should be reminded to take their time. Maintaining body control is very important.

128

RABBIT JUMP

SET UP and MATERIALS:
1. Sufficient mat, rug, or grassy area to accommodate the entire group.
2. Children are barefoot (if indoors).

PROCEDURE:
1. The *teacher* uses one child to demonstrate the "squat position." This position is assumed with the hands placed on the mat (about shoulder distance apart). Both feet are placed between the hands.
2. The RABBIT JUMP means that the hands move forward and both feet follow (*jumping* forward to meet the hands). The pattern continues with hands moving, followed by the feet.
3. Students should keep their feet together and their knees together. Hands should be kept about shoulder distance apart.

SPECIFIC GOAL:
1. *Body awareness*
2. *Bilateral coordination*
3. *Vestibular stimulation*
4. *Dynamic balance*

SUGGESTIONS and VARIATIONS:
1. Initially, the *teacher* should verbally cue the students by saying, "Hands move. Feet move. Hands move. Feet move."

EQUIPMENT

INCHWORM

SET UP and MATERIALS:
1. Sufficient mat, rug, or grassy area to accommodate the entire group.
2. Children are barefoot (if indoors).

PROCEDURE:
1. Demonstrating at first with one child, the *teacher* checks to see that the feet are between the hands with the hands resting palms down on the mat. Knees should be slightly bent.
2. The *teacher* says, "Now, with your feet frozen in place, move only your hands forward in itty, bitty, tiny *walking* steps." The hands should move only as far forward as to maintain good *balance.*
3. Continuing, the *teacher* says, "Now with your hands frozen in place move only your feet as far forward in itty, bitty, tiny *walking* steps." The feet move only as far forward as to meet with the hands.
4. Children move forward toward the destination in this fashion maintaining good *balance* and control.

SPECIFIC GOAL:
1. *Balance*
2. *Body awareness*
3. *Bilateral coordination*
4. *Tactile stimulation*
5. *Vestibular stimulation*

SUGGESTIONS and VARIATIONS:
1. Children should be encouraged to take their time. Maintaining body control is very important.

130

FROG JUMP

SET UP and MATERIALS:
1. Sufficient mat, rug, or grassy area to accommodate the entire group.
2. Children are barefoot (if indoors).

PROCEDURE:
1. With one child, the *teacher* demonstrates the "squat position." This position is assumed with the hands placed on the mat (about shoulder distance apart). Both feet are placed between hands or hands can be placed between feet.
2. The FROG JUMP means that the student "springs" forward from the mat with hands and feet leaving the mat at the same time.
3. The *teacher* should encourage the students to use the balls of their feet for take off and landing.
4. Initially the *teacher* could use a signal (i.e. "ribet") to initiate each FROG JUMP. Once the technique is established, the signal can be eliminated. It is helpful to have a route or pattern to follow.

SPECIFIC GOAL:
1. *Dynamic Balance*
2. *Bilateral coordination*
3. *Kinesthetic awareness*
4. *Vestibular stimulation*

SUGGESTIONS and VARIATIONS:
1. The FROG JUMP should not be confused with the RABBIT JUMP (p. 129).
2. The RABBIT JUMP should not be introduced before the FROG JUMP.
3. Children should be encouraged to take their time.

131

CRAB WALK

SET UP and MATERIALS:
1. Sufficient mat, rug, or grassy area to accommodate the entire group.
2. Children are barefoot (if indoors).

PROCEDURE:
1. The *teacher* tells the children, "We will begin by having everyone make the trunk of their body look like a table. Have your eyes look upward so that your feet and hands are holding up your body."
2. The *teacher* should check each child to see if the body is held straight and flat. The *teacher* can say, "Now, do not let anything drop off your table. Keep your table nice and flat."
3. With either the head or feet leading, the children should move towards a designated destination. A starting signal from the *teacher* is often helpful when the CRAB WALK is first taught.

SPECIFIC GOAL:
1. *Balance*
2. *Body awareness*
3. *Laterality*
4. *Upper body strength*
5. *Vestibular stimulation*

SUGGESTIONS and VARIATIONS:
1. It is important for children to take their time and not rush.

BEAR WALK

SET UP and MATERIALS:
1. Sufficient mat, rug, or grassy area to accommodate the entire group.
2. Children are barefoot (if indoors).

PROCEDURE:
1. The *teacher* asks the children, "Please get down in the DOG WALK (p. 127) position. Your stomach is facing down and the palms of your hands are on the floor."
2. Children will maneuver their bodies forward. The hand and foot from one side of the body are lifted in unison from the mat and move forward before they are set down. Then, the hand and foot from the other side of the body move forward in unison and are set down.

SPECIFIC GOAL:
1. *Unilateral coordination*
2. *Body awareness*
3. *Balance*
4. *Vestibular stimulation*

SUGGESTIONS and VARIATIONS:
1. It is recommended that the DOG WALK (p. 127) be thoroughly mastered before introducing the BEAR WALK. These two movements could easily be confused.

EQUIPMENT

133

GORILLA WALK

SET UP and MATERIALS:
1. Sufficient mat, rug, or grassy area to accommodate the entire group.
2. Children are barefoot (if indoors).
3. Children are sitting in a circle with their legs extended straight out.

PROCEDURE:
1. The *teacher* asks each child to locate their own ankles with their hands.
2. Then, the *teacher* says, "Please stand up. *Bend* over and grasp your ankles with your hands."
3. On a signal from the *teacher*, the children *walk* in this fashion. They should be asked to notice how their feet move with one foot in front of the other in turn. The hands should remain holding the ankles.

SPECIFIC GOAL:
1. *Balance*
2. *Laterality*
3. *Kinesthetic awareness*
4. *Vestibular stimulation*

SUGGESTIONS and VARIATIONS:
1. This skill is difficult for the three to five year old because their arms and legs are still disproportionate.

134

FORWARD ROLL

SET UP and MATERIALS:
1. Sufficient mat space to accommodate the entire group.
2. Children are barefoot.

PROCEDURE:
1. The *teacher* says, "Put one hand on the back of the head." The *teacher* checks to see that each child knows that the back of the head is not the same as the top of the head. Also, the back of the head is not the neck area. Before safely learning how to do a FORWARD ROLL, each child must correctly locate the back of the head.
2. Once it is ascertained that everyone in the group knows the importance of using the back of the head, then, one child is selected to demonstrate while the rest of the group sits in *ready position* and watches carefully. The *teacher* helps that child assume the "squat position," which means that both hands are placed on the mat about shoulder width apart with feet placed between the hands.
3. The *teacher* guides the child as he keeps his hands solidly on the mat, places the back of the head on the mat into this rounded position known as the "tuck position." From, the "tuck position," the child pushes with his toes, lifting the hips upward and keeping the chin tucked against the chest. At this point, the hands also push off and the body rolls forward.
4. The *teacher* should never allow any child's head to touch the mat. Only the back of the head touches the mat.
5. We encourage children to immediately stand up straight and tall with both arms raised above their heads. We call this an "Olympic" finish.

SPECIFIC GOAL:
1. *Balance*
2. *Body awareness*
3. *Gross motor coordination*
4. *Vestibular stimulation*
5. *Tactile stimulation*

SUGGESTIONS and VARIATIONS:
1. It is critically important that the child places only the back of the head on the mat. This is to prevent injuries.

135

HOW TO CLOSE AN ACTIVITY

This could also be called the "cool down" time. Young children need a sense of closure to end an activity. This way they know that one thing has ended so another experience can begin. The following activities have worked well for us.

ANGELS IN THE SNOW:
The *teacher* chooses a soothing instrumental music selection (on record or tape). The *teacher* picks a child to demonstrate. The child lays down on his back. Staying in contact with the surface, the child is instructed to open and close the legs first. During this initial phase, the arms are kept down at the sides. Once a smooth sustained legs-apart legs-together movement is mastered, the arms will move away from and return to the sides of the body also keeping in constant contact with the surface. The *teacher* emphasizes that the arms and legs stay in touch with the surface while there is movement away from and back to the body. Mastery of ANGELS IN THE SNOW is a fine example of *coordination.* Children can repeat this activity.

HEEL-AND-TOE FAIRY WALK:
We tell the children that the HEEL-AND-TOE FAIRY casts a spell on us for a short time. During that time, we must *walk* by placing the heel of one foot touching the toes of the other foot. This is best done with children scattered in the available space. The *teacher* will encourage the children to keep their arms away from their bodies to further challenge the maintenance of *balance.* As children walk randomly in the space they are reminded to avoid contact with anyone else thus reinforcing the concept of *personal space.* We ring a bell or use something similar to indicate that the "spell" is broken and we can proceed to something else.

GYMNASTIC JARGON:
These simple activities are truly "cool down" type exercises and should be performed while sitting down with the legs stretched out together. We suggest a repetition of ten times.
1. KNEE HUG: Drawing both knees up to their chest, children "hug" knees, then, release after a short hold to a count of one, two, three, four, five.
2. HAND-TO-TOE-TOUCHING: Without *bending* their knees, children try to touch their hands to their toes. Feet stay together.
3. TOE TOUCH: Children sit with feet comfortably apart. Their arms are out-stretched to the sides. This activity will use the hand of one side of the body, touching the foot of the opposite side. To accomplish this, the *teacher* should give verbal clues such as, "*Turn,* touch toes, up."

You may discover something else that works better with your children. Children feel more secure with the familiar. We recommend consistency in starting and closing your PLAY POWER time.

INDEX AND HOW TO USE IT

We have planned for this to be a working and useful INDEX for you. Included in CAPITAL LETTERS are titles of all games and activities. As with all pages in PLAY POWER, we encourage you to write in this INDEX and make it personally most helpful for your particular needs.

The important WORDS THAT YOU NEED TO KNOW are *italicized* in this INDEX with the page number that has it's definition.

INDEX

138

GAMES THAT REQUIRE LITTLE OR NO EQUIPMENT

Here are games that you can easily use because they require little or no equipment. These should be "stored" in your head and combined with your talent to provide some spontaneous activities for your students.